Psychological Testing

The essential guide to using and surviving the
most popular recruitment and career
development tests

by Dr Stephanie Jones

HARRIMAN HOUSE LTD
3A Penns Road
Petersfield
Hampshire
GU32 2EW
GREAT BRITAIN

Tel: +44 (0)1730 233870
Fax: +44 (0)1730 233880
Email: enquiries@harriman-house.com
Website: www.harriman-house.com

The first edition, *Psychological Testing for Managers*, was published in Great Britain in 1993, this second edition published in 2010.

Copyright © Harriman House Ltd

ISBN 13: 978-1906659-60-8

British Library Cataloguing in Publication Data
A CIP catalogue record for this book can be obtained from the British Library.

Printed and bound by CPI Antony Rowe, Chippenham, Wiltshire

Many of the tests discussed in this book and mentioned by name are registered or unregistered trademarks, as detailed in the box below (denoted by ™ for an unregistered trademark and ® for a registered trademark). In the book's main text, trademark symbols have been omitted for ease of reading. Details of the tests' trademarks and publishers are set forth, and further information on trademark and copyright requirements of the test publishers regarding these tests can be found on the websites of the applicable test companies.

16PF® is a registered trademark of the Institute for Personality and Ability Testing, Inc (IPAT). IPAT is a wholly owned subsidiary of OPP Ltd.

FIRO-B® is a registered trademark of CPP, Inc. OPP Ltd is licensed to use the trademark in Europe.

Fundamental Interpersonal Relations Orientation – B™ is a trademark of CPP, Inc.

Introduction to Type® is a registered trademark of the Myers-Briggs Type Indicator Trust. OPP Ltd is licensed to use the trademark in Europe.

MBTI®, Myers-Briggs Type Indicator and Myers-Briggs are registered trademarks of the Myers-Briggs Type Indicator Trust. OPP Ltd is licensed to use the trademarks in Europe.

The TKI™ logo is a trademark of CPP, Inc.

Contents

About the Author

Dr Stephanie Jones is Associate Professor of Organizational Behavior at Maastricht School of Management (MSM), and also acts as Academic Co-ordinator for Doctoral Programmes. She gained her PhD from University College London and Bachelor's degree from the London School of Economics.

She has taught on the MBA program of MSM in Maastricht, Kuwait, Egypt, Yemen, China, Vietnam, Rwanda, Ghana, Malawi, Suriname, Peru and Kazakhstan.

Dr Jones previously managed consulting (including recruiting) and training businesses in the UK, Hong Kong, China, India, Australia and Dubai. She has also taught for the Universities of Exeter, Cranfield and Leicester in the UK.

Dr Jones has authored more than 25 books on business and management, including on the subjects of psychology, leadership, culture, recruitment, career development and expatriation.

When not travelling around the world teaching, she spends her time researching and writing from her holiday home and boat in Malta.

Preface to the Second Edition, 2010

Despite the changes in almost every aspect of life as we know it over the last fifteen years, I was pleasantly surprised at how much of *Psychological Testing for Managers* (this book's original title) still seemed to be fresh and contemporary. We have even just been through another recession! The most popular psychological tests are still commonly used, but everything is now online. With this new edition, prompted by Louise Hinchen of Harriman House, I have had the exciting opportunity to bring new tests, and new versions of old tests, to a new generation of human resources managers (personnel is another relic of the 1980s and 1990s), job seekers and other interested parties. Enjoy! (I don't think we said that fifteen years ago, either.)

Dr Stephanie Jones

The Happy Return, Malta, 2010

Preface to the First Edition, 1993

The idea behind this book came from my work in researching and writing about various aspects of the corporate human resources world. Over the last few years I have looked in some detail at executive search and selection, interim management and outplacement, all of which make use of psychological testing as a tool to help match people to particular jobs and career opportunities. Psychological testing is increasingly common in the workplace. As a result, I wanted to find out more about it, especially about the different tests, how they are used and what they reveal.

However, all the books that I could find about occupational psychology, and psychological and psychometric testing, were written by professional psychologists, and seemed full of technical jargon and incomprehensible detail. These books were largely about models and theories of personality. They referred occasionally to specific tests, but without explaining what they were like, either from the point of view of the person being tested, or the user of tests.

If you knew you would have to undergo psychological tests in order to be selected for a job, or as part of an appraisal for promotion or transfer, wouldn't you want to know what the tests might entail? If you had not done a test before, you might feel at a disadvantage to someone who had.

Similarly, personnel managers or human resources directors without a background in psychology may be interested in using psychological tests, but have hesitated in the past through lack of knowledge. Many employers know very little about the range of tests available and depend either on second-hand recommendations or opt for the most commonly used tests without an awareness of the alternatives. Training courses are available but may be inconvenient, time-consuming or expensive.

I would like to emphasise that *Psychological Testing for Managers* is absolutely *not* the last word on the subject, but is an introduction for the non-psychologist, both as testee and user. It looks at a selection of the most commonly used tests in non-technical language and in a novel format, explaining what the tests involve, when they should be used, and how they can be combined with other tests to give a well-rounded picture of a potential employees' strengths and weaknesses.

I have also tried to give the reader a feel for what it is like to do these tests. To achieve this, I have taken all the tests myself, and with some I have explained the nature of the feedback in terms of my own results. After the final test, I was told that I was suffering from test-overload, and that the value of doing any more was now limited so I would not recommend any individual to do more than a few tests in close succession.

One of my first experiences of professional writing – more than 10 years ago – was as a restaurant critic, and sometimes I've jokingly referred to this book as 'The Egon Ronay Guide to Psychological Testing'. I certainly hope it will introduce you to the variety and the benefits of psychological testing, whether you are a potential user of tests, or have – or expect to have — experience of them as a candidate for a job or promotion.

If *Psychological Testing for Managers* creates a feeling of familiarity with the concepts, banishes anxiety, allows for critical comparison and provokes interest in the wider subject of occupational psychology, then this book's goals will have been achieved.

Choosing the Psychological Tests for this Book

The tests examined here represent a variety of categories and approaches with a particular focus on intelligence and personality assessments. Among the most established and respected are the Watson Glaser Critical Thinking test, Raven's Progressive Matrices, the Cattell 16PF and the Myers-Briggs Type Indicator. They are still widely used and have many long-term, loyal adherents. PAPI and OPQ are relatively recent developments, the latter created by SHL as a new range of tests for the management market, and must be welcomed as a major step forward in user-friendliness.

I selected these tests by talking to a number of occupational psychologists, and asking them which ones they thought were most commonly encountered. The tests included here are all widely available in the UK, the USA and parts of continental Europe. A number of them, especially the OPQ and PAPI, have also been translated into foreign languages. If you think that an especially important or useful test has been left out, please write to me and tell me about it.

Dr Stephanie Jones

Covent Garden, London, 1993

Foreword

In this invaluable new edition of *Psychological Testing*, my friend and colleague, Dr Stephanie Jones, has tried to help the non-specialist reader to prepare to use psychological tests in a clear, systematic and practical way. With her extensive experience in recruitment and HR consulting, her background in executive training, and her excellent teaching experience with our MBA and DBA students in areas such as Organisational Behaviour, Cross-cultural Management, Leadership, and Behavioural Sciences, Dr Jones fully understands user needs.

Given her expertise, she has produced a user-friendly guide to psychological testing in the workplace. Having tried and tested each of the psychological tests in this book herself, she offers her own detailed comments, aimed at taking away the fear of psychological testing and giving more confidence to the job seeker.

As academic behavioural scientists, we appreciate the importance of psychological testing in aligning employees and jobs. While many of the most popular tests have been used for decades, and have their roots in the nineteenth century, recent research in the field is producing innovative approaches to established psychological testing techniques, which can give us valuable new insights. As academics we must not forget the importance of making our work accessible to the general reader who has practical reasons for using psychological testing, but who might lack the background to understand reports on the psychometric qualities of the tests. With a clear focus on practical use, this book is not intended to be the last word on the psychometric qualities of each specific test; rather it is designed to help the reader looking for a useful starting point to find out more about psychological testing. Moreover, the book points the reader towards additional resources, including opportunities to practice tests online.

Psychological tests can be a very valuable tool but they must be used and interpreted carefully and correctly. This practical introduction can be an important first step in professional psychological test usage. Much of my own academic research has been in the field of careers and employability of workers. Knowing more about yourself and/or about your subordinates' (personality) profiles, using the carefully selected psychological tests included in this book, can be a good beginning in a process that is aimed at changing and developing your career. Obviously, in order to draw accurate conclusions on the use of specific tests, it is highly important to ask for expert advice on the psychometric qualities of the instruments used. After all, psychological testing may have profound implications for employees' careers, and should be undertaken using high ethical standards.

Professor Beatrice van der Heijden
Radboud University Nijmegen, Open University of the Netherlands and University of Twente

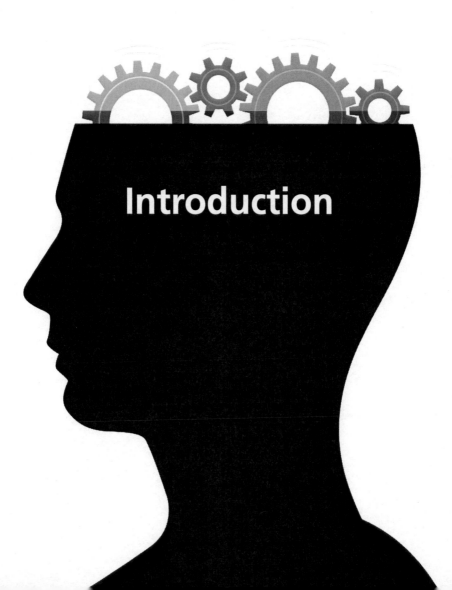

Introduction

Note: The world of psychological testing attributes specific meanings to specific words. Words highlighted in this section the first time they appear, such as **abstract**, are explained in the Glossary.

We all realise that, fundamentally, everyone is different. We all know people who seem to be a world away from ourselves: in their ideas, their appearance and in the way that they go about doing things. It is these differences that make people interesting and that allow us to learn from each other as we go through life. Wouldn't it be boring it everyone was the same?

It is these differences, too, which make it worthwhile for a person to look for a change in job or career, or for a company or organisation to employ someone new, so that they can bring fresh ideas or a new style of operation to a job. But it is also these differences which may mean that the job or career a person chooses is successful or not. The person the company employs may or may not be the right person for the job.

This concern is heard time and again. Letting people go is damaging and traumatic, so we have to get it right first time, and keep getting it right. Job changers are similarly cautious. A job is a precious thing, even if it has a lot of negatives, so it is important to really think about whether you are right for this new job or whether you should stay where you are?

Thus **psychometric** or psychological testing has become a vital tool in the task of minimising risk on all sides in recruitment and in career management decisions. As more and more employers use psychological testing, more and more people in the workplace will find themselves being tested, but which psychological **test**(s) should be used, in which circumstances, and why?

Which test?

This book, unlike most others on psychological testing, lists a series of tests in order to provide you – a person about to undergo psychological testing, or a potential user of tests on your own executives, managers and job candidates – with a brief introduction to a range of popular tests used frequently in a variety of organisations. It has been written with these scenarios – among others – in mind:

Testee

- You have applied for a job and, at the first interview, you are told by the headhunter or agency that the prospective employer is quite interested in you, but their practice is to put everyone through the Watson Glaser Critical Thinking Analysis. You haven't heard of this and have no idea what it might entail.

- You are approached by a headhunter and agree to discuss a possible job opportunity. The headhunter insists that in order to go on to the next stage you must undergo a battery (i.e. combination) of short psychological tests. You don't know what this means, and you don't know the names of any popular, short psychological (or less common and longer) tests to ask if these will be included.

- You are being considered for promotion to a different position in the company. It is agreed that you have the qualifications and experience to do the job, but your boss is concerned about whether you will 'fit in' with the new team. They have already gone through the Belbin Team Roles exercise and you must go through it too. What is it? Should you be worried about it?

User

- You are the manager of a small, entrepreneurial group developing new products for the parent company. It has been suggested that you should expand your operations and recruit two new members of staff, who must be self-starting, creative, risk-taking and decisive. You've heard about the use of psychological tests in selection and feel this could help here, but which test should you use?

- You are the managing director of a well-established, medium-sized company about to retire after 15 years in the job, having built the business from scratch. You have created a group of mangers to run a division of the business and would like one of them to succeed you, but which one? Who has the necessary vision and leadership to take over?

- You have just started working in a small recruitment consultancy, and one of the clients asks that all candidates for his assignment should undergo a series of psychological tests. He doesn't know much about these and wants you to advise him. What do you say?

How to use the test summaries

This book looks at a range of popular psychological tests, which I have analysed and discussed in such a way as to help you answer the questions above. Other benefits include:

Testee

- If you are told that you are about to be given a certain psychological test, you can read about it and mentally prepare yourself.

- If you are told you are to be presented with a battery of tests, you can quote the names of some of the short tests described here, e.g. OPQ, PAPI, Myers Briggs, 16PF and FIRO-B, and ask if any of these are on the agenda. The odds are that at least one will be. The SHL OPQ is particularly popular as part of a battery of tests.

User

- If you need to find a certain test which show up specific qualities in individuals, you can look up the descriptions of a number of the tests to see which might be most suitable.

- If you need to recommend the use of specific tests to another person, you can discuss the most popular tests available, how they can be combined and quote the experiences of other users.

Presentation of the test summaries

The tests are presented here in a uniform format to help answer the most commonly-asked questions, from the point of view of both the **testee** and the **user**. This is based on the background to the design of the test, its aims, format and uses or applications, what it's like to do, examples of what the test looks like, time needed for taking the test, scoring and feedback, with comments on uses and value.

Background
This describes the origins of the test and examines its usage, popularity and **norms**.

The aims of the test
This itemises the aspects of aptitude, **personality** and/or ability being tested in each case.

The format
This basically describes what the test looks like, and how it is likely to be presented to you as a testee. The aim is to familiarise you with its format and offset the 'fear of the unknown'. For example, is the test **ipsative** or not?

Range of applications
This lists the ways in which the test can be used, particularly in terms of recruitment selection, career development, etc., for the user.

Doing the test
This tells you, as the testee, what it's like to actually do each test. It was written immediately after each one was administered, and

conveys my first impressions as well as more detailed reflections and comparisons with other tests.

Examples of content of the test

Wherever possible this section quotes actual extracts from the test. If you have not done tests before, it should help you to gain a certain amount of prior experience. Most of these tests are not easily available, and in most cases can only be sold to qualified psychologists.

Time needed to complete the test

This gives an approximate idea of how long most people take to do the test. It is useful when putting together batteries of tests and estimating scheduling times for users, and gives guidelines to those completing the test for the first time.

Time to score the test

This is helpful for the user in choosing tests that are based on the speed of obtaining results. It is necessary to know this if you want a test which can be administered, scored and the results presented to the person being tested on the same occasion. As a testee, can you reasonably expect to be given the results of the test on the spot? Computer-generated feedback is usually available instantly.

Necessary time for feedback

This is also useful for an employer or headhunter to know when scheduling a number of people to be tested, and for the person being tested. How long does the entire exercise take? Everyone being tested should insist on feedback, and knowing the average time it takes to receive that feedback on a particular test can assure you, as a testee, that you have received more, or less, feedback than usual. Computer-generated feedback is, of course, standardised and may be less useful as a result.

Format/structure of the feedback

This indicates the topics that will generally be covered in the feedback. This is a useful indication of the content of the test, and can help the user to decide if this test is appropriate for a particular use; it also helps you as the testee to know what to expect. If you feel that you are not receiving adequate feedback, then this section helps you to suggest other areas to cover.

Value to the employer/user

This summarises the value of a particular test for the user, in terms of the qualities being tested and occupational applications.

Value to the employee/person being tested

This summarises how the test helps you, as the testee, to understand your qualities in the context of the situation for which you are being tested. As an applicant if you are unsuccessful then you should still insist on receiving feedback, so that you can gain the benefit of having undergone a psychological test which might tell you something new about yourself. You might learn something which can help you in future job hunts.

Value to the user organisation

This section in particular looks at the value of the test in determining the suitability of a person for a specific corporate culture. Here, the test will be discussed in terms of how the person will fit into a 'macho' culture, a 'process' culture, a 'retail' culture, and a 'high-risk, slow-feedback' culture (discussed further below).

Can the test results be deliberately falsified?

In most cases, you will find that test results cannot be falsified, and even if they can, then the fact that they were falsified will be discovered sooner or later, to the detriment of the relationship between the employer and employee.

Of course, it is pointless trying to present yourself as having characteristics other than those you genuinely have. Many tests have built-in consistency measures, so deliberate falsification becomes quite obvious to the test administrator.

Advantages over other tests
This looks at why a particular test is preferred by users and those being tested for certain qualities, including speed of being administered, **validity**, the extent of validation, etc.

Disadvantage compared with other tests
This looks at the drawbacks of each test. There is certainly no such thing as the 'perfect' test, and this is why a battery of tests can be particularly valuable.

Tests may be combined with...
This suggests combinations of popular tests for specific purposes. Some tests stand up well on their own for a variety of applications, while others confirm or question the results of other tests. In most circumstances, especially in recruitment and selection, tests will be presented to candidates in a group rather than singly.

Static/predictive value
This indicates the value of the test in describing the attributes of the person being tested at the point in time when the testing exercise takes place, compared with how useful it is in indicating how the person being tested will behave in the future. Different tests have different degrees of usefulness in predicting future behaviour.

Overall review
This summarises the basic features of each test.

How to prepare yourself for sitting this test

This suggests what you should do if you are taking the test for the first time. It cannot tell you how to affect the results of the test to fit in with the impression you want to convey; on the contrary, it warns against attempting this. Instead, it suggests how you should mentally prepare yourself for answering the questions as frankly as possible so that the test can be of maximum benefit to both parties.

Will this test produce a different result after a period of time?

This section looks at the shelf-life of each test according to the results produced about one individual, suggesting when it could be repeated. If you are being tested for a particular job or promotion then you may have done that test before. If you did it less than six months ago, then the results are probably still valid. If it was much more than a year ago then you may well have to retake it.

As a testee, you should always insist on having a copy of your test results in case this happens. It can be useful for employers to know how long the results of a test are valid when planning career development. Some tests can only be done once, as part of the test is the novelty of doing them. Experiencing them a second time would lose this unique value.

The best way of using this book is to derive an overview of the most popular tests, and then look at individual tests in detail as required, either as a testee or user. Further information on particular tests can be obtained from the books listed in Further Reading (p.221), and by contacting the organisations listed on page 227.

Psychology at work

Management theorists have, for many years, argued that effective management is only possible through an understanding of employees' personalities and behavioural styles, as well as their working situations. Research also shows that a 'person-centred' rather than 'production-centred' management style produces better, and more effective, business results in the long term.

Therefore, in the field of personnel selection, team-building and career development, identifying the way in which an employee differs from others, is considered important. To do this we need tools which will allow us to look at different aspects of personality, and which will give us an indication of how someone is likely to react in certain circumstances. If they are under stress, or in a situation which demands a high level of tact and diplomacy, they may behave differently. In short, what we need is a model or series of models which can be used to help managers understand their employees better and adjust their management style accordingly.

Personality tests which use sound psychological methods can provide managers with information relating to basic aspects of personality, so that predictions about behaviour can be made with a fair degree of confidence, including **competence** and **motivation**. This information is important when a company or organisation is making decisions about the recruitment, appraisal or development of staff, or needs to form new teams for specific tasks.

To be effective, successful and reasonably satisfied in their working environment, managers must be able to come to terms with their own psychology and that of their colleagues. If you are a senior manager, you must be able to use this knowledge and these insights to make appropriate hiring and promotion decisions.

Psychological testing will enable you to have some understanding of how you relate to others, and of how others relate to you. The age of the lone-ranger executive or manager is long over, and effectiveness is now about being able to work in teams, in almost every workplace situation.

An understanding of psychology and of psychological **profiles** should therefore be a vital ingredient in any senior manager's repertoire. This will become increasingly important as the competitive environment facing most organisations becomes more and more sophisticated.

The theories behind occupational psychology

Since the first personality tests were developed, different theories have formed the basis for specific personality tests. Typically, psychological/psychometric models of personality have identified a number of core personality traits, with the number of traits identified by any particular theory varying from two to sixteen, and in a few cases even more.

One of the earliest theories of personality, now very well known and widely adopted, is the two-factor model proposed by H. J. Eysenck in 1947. He argued that the major sources of individual personality difference could be reduced to two basic factors, each of which operated independently of the other. The first of these two factors was *Introversion* vs. *Extroversion*, and the second, *Stability* vs. *Neuroticism*. To a large extent, many personality tests on the market today relate to these basic findings of Eysenck, which in turn make use of a number of the insights of Jung and Freud.

So how did early psychologists arrive at their theories of personality? Eysenck, for example, discovered his model by gathering responses to questions about a large number of personality variables. This showed that several apparently different personality traits seemed to cluster together: an individual who scored highly on, say, acting impulsively and risk-taking would also tend to score highly on sociability and activity. To Eysenck, this implied that there was some common factor underlying these specific personality traits.

Eysenck's model, however, provided only a limited insight into human personality. Many felt that a more sophisticated model was needed, and other researchers began to produce them, ultimately leading to the creation of many of the well-known personality tests on the market today.

Warning for potential users

As the use of psychological testing has become more widespread and users have become more familiar with testing techniques, there has been a growing concern that, instead of using tests as a way of adding value to other management information sources, many users are taking advantage of the easy and inexpensive availability of psychological tests as a quick fix in their human resources decisions. Companies are sometimes using tests as a substitute for making carefully thought-through management decisions rather than as an aid to such careful thinking.

It cannot be emphasised too strongly that psychological tests can only aid and inform management judgement; they cannot replace it. Managers are not absolved from making difficult or easy selection and/or promotion decisions through the use of psychological tests, however skilfully they are **interpreted**. Psychological tests should never be used as a means of letting managers off the hook in making difficult choices.

Many psychologists suggest that a battery of tests can be used provided that the client is prepared to use them as part of a systematic procedure that includes a number of steps and stages, with built-in checks and balances. The client must take the time to understand the tests and what they attempt to achieve, which is often limited. The client must also be prepared to allocate the time and money for adequate explanation and feedback, whether they are successful in the selection process or not.

Psychological testing should be seen as part of the wider and continuing process of seeking to understand individuals in the context of career development and team-building, to show strengths and weaknesses, and areas for future attention. They should not be used solely for selection and then put away in the filing cabinet and eventually, inevitably, shredded. For existing employees, tests taken at various stages of their careers will always provide important insights. Recruitment and selection is only part of an employee's experience and contribution to an organisation.

What tests say about an employer

It can be revealing for prospective – or existing – employees to critically examine their company's choice and use of psychological tests. Which particular tests do they prefer? Do they tend to use just one or two, or several? Are they modified or entirely changed from time to time, or is there a long tradition of using only tried and tested **instruments**? Are controlled and user-friendly conditions provided for those undergoing the tests? Most importantly, how much preliminary information and post-test feedback is provided? Are the employees given a copy of their interpreted results, and assured that any other copies are confidentially and securely locked away?

A company's attitude to psychological testing reveals much about how progressive, caring and committed they are to the importance of their human resource assets. This insight can be very useful in helping a prospective employee to decide whether or not to join a company, and those administering the tests should be aware of this.

Ideally, a company using psychological testing as a recruitment and development procedure will, in the process, heighten its employees' perceptions of its care and approach to developing management excellence. When a company has to make a decision between candidates for a position, and when it is clear that they cannot all be successful, those who are turned away – or, preferably, come to an agreement that this specific opportunity is not for them at this particular time – should retain a favourable impression of the organisation.

A well-chosen battery of psychological tests – with extensive feedback for each test-taker – combined with a thoughtfully conducted personal interview, will achieve this objective, with both successful and unsuccessful candidates coming away from the experience feeling positive. Selection procedures should be carefully designed to fit the job and the characteristics of the person being sought.

It should never be forgotten that the recruitment process is also all about marketing the company, in public relations terms. The most sensitive PR audience for any company is the group of people who were unsuccessful in applying for jobs there: what will they say about the company in the market place? They will certainly have an opinion, and the employer should go to some lengths to ensure that it is an accurate – and overall, positive – one.

Going for a job is very much a two-way process, and the unsuccessful applicants will take away with them an impression of how they were handled that cannot be rectified later. It can be easy for them to badmouth the company and justify their rejection, especially if HR processes are poor. Psychological testing can be an important part of these processes.

Companies with long traditions of using psychological testing enjoy the cumulative benefits of having built up a large databank of normative data, based on a past population of test-takers, and can develop a picture of their 'employee most likely to succeed' against a given job specification. This encourages clarity and disciplined thinking about matching people with jobs. The careful use of well-chosen psychological tests has become, over the last half-century, the hallmark of a good employer.

The acceptability of psychological tests

Some of the tests most favoured by many employers and candidates are not deemed scientifically valid or reliable by psychologists. Some tests are well–received because of their strong face validity – or user-friendliness – and are often very useful as a counselling tool, even though they are not seen as valid in a scientific sense.

It is important to remember the distinctions between scientific validity, scientific reliability and face validity. Tests which are scientifically valid and reliable can lack face validity and thus appear pointless. If no one wants to do the test because it seems to be a waste of time and they can't see the thinking behind it, it has failed the public relations test, however scientifically proven it may be.

The acceptability of psychological tests has increased greatly through the use of computer technology, and the effect of this on the candidate-tester relationship. The tester is no longer the person who administers and scores the test; instead, he or she is the person who explains the point of it at the outset, and debriefs afterwards. The candidate is interacting with the computer screen, which then helps them to come to terms with the tester as an objective party.

Much of the traditional fear of psychologists, especially in the British context, stemmed originally from the 1940s War Office procedure of sending all officer candidates for 'an interview with the psychologist'. This was interpreted by many to mean **psychiatrist**, and therefore 'shrink'. Even now, the distinction between the two is imperfectly understood. The fear of being mentally undressed by this individual was particularly heightened by the characteristic British sense of reserve (not unknown to many other cultures), provoking a typical 'stiff-upper-lip' reaction. The psychologist/psychiatrist was not seen as a human being just doing his or her job, but as a holder of secret weapons which would be used to lay bare the defenceless individual's inner soul. There was no hiding place!

The widespread use of computer technology in psychological testing has helped to mitigate this legacy of fear and apprehension. The candidate uses various computer programs to gain self-knowledge, and then sees the psychologist afterwards, who will help with the interpretation. The psychologist's role is developmental, not judgmental. The computer has liberated the candidate to remain a person, and liberated the psychologist to be a counsellor. Those readers now in their twenties and thirties might find this difficult to imagine.

Matching people to company cultures

It is important to bear in mind models of company cultures when assessing psychological tests and the types of personality they define. One of the principal purposes of using psychological testing effectively is to select people to work in certain cultures, or to understand why people are effective or not effective in their existing company. The model of company cultures outlined here has been used to appraise the value of certain psychological tests in the following test summaries, especially in terms of looking at the 'value of the test to the user organisation'.

There are many models of company cultures but the following simple model of four types from the Ashridge Management College is useful. This classifies all companies into four types:

1. The **macho** culture;

2. The **process** culture;

3. The **retail** culture;

4. The **high-risk, slow-feedback** culture.

The macho culture attracts individualistic, high-risk operators who like quick feedback of their results; people who will find a mountain and climb it. Many consultancies and advertising agencies have macho cultures, and this group would also include magazine companies and newspaper companies.

Process cultures include local authorities and capital goods manufacturers; companies in which technical expertise is very important. Process cultures are concerned with how the work is done and attention to detail, and often the customer and end-users are not particularly important. The method of working, however, is all important, and people in process cultures tend to focus on the actual process of their work.

In a retail culture, people work hard and play hard, and are very customer-driven. This culture favours fast action but low risk with frenetic activity selling high-demand products, such as hamburgers: for example McDonald's. There are strict, specifically laid–down rules; decision-making is easy, and feedback is rapid.

This is in considerable contrast with a high-risk, slow-feedback culture such as the aircraft industry, and design-oriented capital goods companies such as Rolls Royce. It can take seven or eight years of research to create a new aircraft engine, and even then someone else might make a better one. It can take a long time to find out if the decisions made will turn out to have been the right ones.

It is essential to consider these company culture differences when matching people to job roles. Each psychological test considered here is examined in terms of its value in indicating the extent to which a person will or will not fit into a specific organisational culture. See, under each test, the section entitled 'Value of the Test to the User Organisation'.

Other models of organisational culture should also be considered, such as Charles Handy's plus others quoted in Organisational Behaviour textbooks (see Further Reading). Are people comfortable in a Power culture dominated by a spider in a web; or in a Role culture, with strong departmental pillars? Do they prefer task-based work, or an organisation revolving around them as an individual? Looking at the issue in a different way, are they attracted to a market-driven or entrepreneurial culture? Or do they feel more comfortable in a clan-culture or bureaucracy?

It might also be argued that national cultures should be considered in understanding psychology. This is a large and important topic, addressed to a certain extent by the developing of different language editions of tests and of norm groups of test-takers among specific nationalities. For example, although frequency of extraversion and introversion in national populations does not vary, the expression of this characteristic can be very different. The extraverts in the USA are more extreme than in Japan or China; by contrast, the introverts in Japan or China are more extreme in the way they express themselves than introverts in the USA. Different nationalities have differing values. For example, some would consider conflict as positive and productive, others see conflict as negative and in terms of their values would seek harmony at any cost. While some nationalities support values involving risk-taking, others are risk-averse. Much of the study of psychology is based on an assumption of a degree of individualism among test-takers. Personalities are constant across cultures, but some societies are community-oriented in their values, do not encourage individualism, and exhibit pressure to conform. Clearly, this is a subject for wider investigation, outside of the scope of the present book.

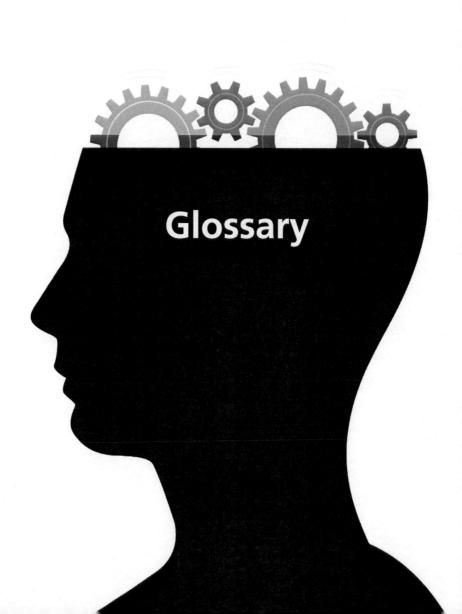

Glossary

Occupational psychology comes with its own special jargon. This section defines and describes the words highlighted in the introduction (such as **abstract**) and many others mentioned during the test summaries. This glossary is intended to offer a brief, basic explanation of words occurring in the book which may not be familiar to non-psychologists. More detailed definitions may be obtained by consulting the books listed under Further Reading at the end of the book.

For the person being tested, it will help you to become aware of the buzz words used in the world of occupational psychology. You don't want to be fazed by hearing these words and not knowing what they mean. For the inexperienced user, these definitions will certainly help you to pin-point the characteristics of different tests. The more savvy psychologist can use this listing as an aide-mémoire and for quick reference when required.

ABSTRACT

Used in the expression 'abstract reasoning', as opposed to verbal and numerical reasoning. 'Abstract', as a concept, is concerned with the representation of ideas in geometrical and other designs. A person being asked to undertake an abstract test is, by definition, being asked to establish relationships and recognise patterns between entirely different, only similar, or the same geometrical designs.

APPLICATIONS

As in 'applications of psychological tests'. 'Application' as a concept can include the use of psychological tests in selection, induction, team-building and career development, as well as in crisis intervention. Most of the tests reviewed in this book are concerned with recruitment. However, besides recruitment, applications are principally designed for improving performance and communication skills, and fitting employees with promotion opportunities.

CLINICAL

Clinical psychology is concerned with observation and strictly objective applications in the field of the mental well-being of patients. Clinical psychology looks particularly at the resolution of internal conflicts experienced by patients. Occupational psychology, as the name suggests, is more related to the workplace, and also must be objective and scientific.

COMPETENCE

This is concerned with fitness, efficiency, capacity and sufficiency. Competencies are seen in middle-management terms as highly specific measurable features, whereas in senior management there is a greater concern with capacity more than competency. The concept of competency is thus much more nebulous at the senior level. Competence is specifically defined by occupational psychologists as utilising and facilitating the use of resources to maximum effect in three areas: managing resources and systems; sensitivity to the environment and external factors; and personal effectiveness.

FEEDBACK

This refers to the opportunity to discuss and explore the results of a person's assessment, considering them in terms of the implications for suitability for a particular job or promotion, and various aspects of the individual's personal and occupational development.

INDEX

This refers statistically to a comparison between a number of variables, but psychologically it is often used as an indicator of certain features within a personality.

INDICATOR

This reference to features of a personality is less specific than 'test results'. 'Indication', by contrast, marks basic preferences and tendencies. The MBTI is known as an indicator of types.

INSTRUMENT

This is simply another name for a test, in so far as it is a tool used to measure specific elements – in this case of a personality.

INTERPRETATION

This refers to making sense of results in the context of psychological tests and understanding those test results in terms of the necessary applications. Tests can be interpreted in a variety of ways according to the context, and the needs of the user and testee.

INVENTORY

This implies a listing of features rather than an assessment or test. An inventory is more objective and less judgmental than a test.

IPSATIVE

This refers to a test which includes multiple-choice questions, and the sum of all the options expressed adds up to a constant. The opposite of ipsative is normative, which is looking for indications to compare against a specific norm group.

LIKERT SCALE

This is a way of collecting feedback on a statement, usually with five options, ranging from "completely dissatisfied" to "completely satisfied". It is used in the SHL Motivation Questionnaire. These options are usually phrased as "completely agree", "generally agree", "neutral", "generally disagree", "completely disagree", etc.

MODE

This describes the way a person operates according to how they react to a given situation. Some people operate in a variety of modes, while others are more restricted in the way they behave. This can relate to 'Mode of Conflict', for example. These modes are competing, collaborating, compromising, accommodating and avoiding – they are ways of describing the manner in which a person prefers to operate.

MOTIVATION

This has been classified in a number of ways, and has been defined in terms of three elements by the famous occupational psychologist, David McClelland: the need for achievement, the need for affiliation, and the need for power. More generally, the word motivation is used to describe aptitude and keenness, especially in terms of self-motivation.

NORMS

This relates to the types of respondents and the ordering of the most frequent value or state. People should be compared against their norm group, i.e. people like themselves. The word normal comes from this word, and implies the reflection of a standard against which one is compared. Breaking the norm is seen as being outside of one's usual group.

OCCUPATIONAL

This relates to one's job and one's working environment and, in the expression 'occupational psychology', is used in contrast to clinical psychology. Occupational psychology is concerned with studying people who are employed or occupied in a craft, trade or profession, and examines their behaviour and the reasons for this behaviour whilst in the workplace.

PERCENTILES

This refers to the value below which a specified percentage may fall. If all individuals are ranked in groups of the highest and lowest, according to raw scores, the percentile rank of a particular individual is a percentage of the total group who are ranked below this individual. If we are told that a person's percentile rank on a test is 22, we know that person scored higher than 22 per cent of the people taking the test.

PERSONALITY

This summarises the nature of a person's existence in terms of his or her individual, distinctive and well-marked characteristics. Personality refers to an integration of all the psychological, intellectual, emotional and physical characteristics of an individual, especially according to how it is presented to other people in terms of behaviour and attitudes.

POPULATION

A population is a group which the testee represents. The following are examples of populations: managerial and professional people who live in the UK; people who work for Microsoft. Samples or norm groups are chosen to represent their populations. For example, several thousand people could be chosen to represent the UK in terms of age, gender, race, employment status, etc. Population also refers to the people in a class considered statistically together.

PREDICTIVE

This means a test relating to the future behaviour of a person. Some tests are static, i.e. describing only present features, whereas predictive tests say something about how an individual might behave in a given situation, even if this has not been encountered before.

PROFILE

This means a summary or short biographical sketch, and is used generally by psychologists in bringing out the main characteristics of their tests, such as the DMT Profile or the Insight Profile, for example, in describing a person.

PSYCHOANALYSIS

This is the investigation of psychological forces making up a personality, as originally defined by Sigmund Freud in the nineteenth century. This includes the theory that the mind can be divided into conscious or subconscious elements.

PSYCHODYNAMIC

This pertains to mental and emotional forces, including those from past experience, and their effects on the present. The DMT is a psychodynamic test.

PSYCHOLOGY

Basically, this is the science of the mind. Psychological testing is a broader concept than psychometric testing, encompassing a number of varieties of psychological tests. The DMT may be seen as a psychological test, as it does not include metrics or numerical scores. Many other tests reviewed here are psychometric – see below.

PSYCHOMETRIC

This is branch of psychology dealing with measurable factors, which can be clearly and specifically calculated, and the person given a numerical score. This is not to be confused with psychometry, the measurement of the duration of mental processes and the faculty of divining an unknown person's qualities by handling objects used by them.

QUESTIONNAIRE

This refers to a type of test which includes a series of questions, usually for the respondent to make a series of comparisons. A questionnaire result usually shows a variety of features and attitudes of the respondent, rather than testing particular abilities, which would require more vocationally-based instruments. Questionnaires are usually self-reported, where the person completing the questionnaire – the testee – considers their own attitudes to each of the questions. In this book, the word 'test' is widely used, where strictly speaking, 'questionnaire' or 'assessment' or 'inventory' might be more accurate.

RAW SCORE

This is the basic score before being converted into percentiles against the norm group.

RESPONSE

The testing of a person's reaction to a given situation or stimuli; this is the main feature for which psychological tests have been designed to examine. Some psychological testing companies call testees 'respondents'.

RESULTS

The scored, finalised features of a test, which may contain numerical elements, as presented in the feedback session to the individual.

SCORING

The appraisal of test results according to the aim of the test, and according to the norm group.

STATIC

As opposed to predictive tests, static tests look at a person's behaviour now rather than in the future. Sometimes they are indicative of future behaviour, sometimes they are not.

STEN SCORE

This is a way of scoring results according to an index, from 1 to 10, in specific psychometric tests which look at gradations and degrees of a certain type of behaviour. For example, a respondent could be a 7 on anxiety and 6 on friendliness. The term 'sten score' indicates and is a short form for 'Standardised Ten'.

TEST

The word 'test' is generally used in this book as synonymous with questionnaire, assessment, inventory or instrument, but specifically it means 'trial of fitness for examination'. A test is a specific way of examining the existence, or lack of, certain indicators through asking questions. There is often a clear link between the choices made by the respondent and the measurable outcomes. The use of the word 'test' is not necessarily widely accepted in the psychology community because of the implications of producing right or wrong answers. Here, as in the title of the book, it is used for convenience and as a general expression.

TESTEE

Used in this book as the person being tested. This is not necessarily the client, who might be paying for the testing services – see User, below. Most psychological testing firms do not use this term, but talk about 'respondents' or 'participants' or another such term. Here, it has evolved from the use of 'coach' and 'coachee'.

TESTER

Refers to the person administering the test who may be a professional psychologist, but who also may hold a licence from the psychological testing providing company, and has been trained in administering products. Thus testers can be in-house (in the organisation using the testing services on their staff) or out-house (at the testing providing company).

TYPES

Another word for categories; used here to identify elements of personality and collect them together into certain defined groups. It also can be used to refer to behaviour types, as in the Belbin Team Roles.

USER

Used in this book to signify the employer such as a Human Resources staff member who requests the tests to be carried out, or an executive search firm who conducts psychological tests on behalf of their clients. Basically, the user is the client of the psychological testing company and the person who buys the test.

VALIDITY

This relates to the effectiveness, adequacy and substantiated nature of a test. Face validity is an expression concerning the way the test appears to the testee. A test with high face validity looks to the testee like a meaningful exercise with relevant questions. A test with low face validity can be rejected by suspicious and unconvinced testees.

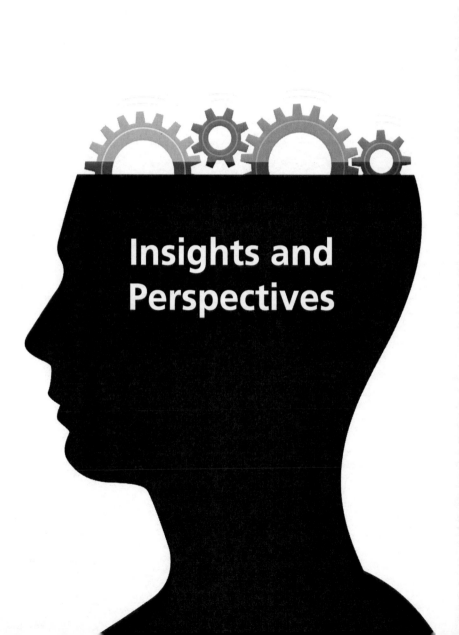

Insights and
Perspectives

The insights presented here are included to explain why certain tests have been chosen for coverage in this book, in terms of:

- Their usefulness and popularity among users.

- The perspectives of the psychologists designing these tests.

- What it feels like (as a testee) to do the test and receive feedback.

- How academic psychologists view these tests and their usage.

Considerable research was carried out in all these categories, and by people with the experience of psychological testing to decide upon the tests selected here.

These perspectives are intended to introduce the particular tests chosen, and to raise a number of important issues, seen as concerns by users, testers, testees and Specialists. These issues are not pursued in depth: it must be emphasised that this book is an introductory guide prepared for non-Specialists by a former user and academic but non-Specialist, and does not intend to go into the detail with which professional and academic psychologists are concerned.

Users' perspectives

A user of psychological testing (large financial services organisation)

This user of psychological tests is constantly being approached by testing companies offering their services. He has extensive needs for testing, so their approaches are not without justification. But he finds it difficult to decide between the tests being offered, and needs to be convinced of their practical value before proceeding to use them on an extensive scale. He has found a number of them to be particularly suitable (especially the OPQ, DMT, Myers Briggs and PAPI) and discusses them below.

"We have quite a few problems with some of our young traders and analysts. We invest a lot of time and effort in training them, only to find that they either leave us and go elsewhere, or that they are basically rather unstable, can't stand the pace and burn out. I have been particularly impressed by the value of the DMT in predicting which of our young traders will make it. This test was developed to identify potentially successful fighter pilots for the Swedish Air Force, and I guess that there are relatively few differences between being a successful combat pilot and being a successful stockbroker. You must have cool nerves, good judgement, emotional stability and belief in yourself.

"We have substantially improved our track record in developing young brokers through the DMT. We still lose people to competitors, but at least now we are able to identify those who will or won't make it. Those who don't appear to have the drive, or lack emotional security, or who are contemptuous of authority and rock the boat too much in the office, are weeded out before appointment. We have also used the DMT on existing staff, and then deploy them as appropriate. Using the DMT widely throughout the organisation has proved expensive, but it has saved us from making some more expensive mistakes.

"We also use more conventional psychological tests, such as OPQ, PAPI and Myers Briggs and these help us a great deal in team-building. We are part of a Japanese multinational and Japanese management techniques tend to revolve around teams. We use psychological tests to determine which of the people we consider for appointment are most appropriate for the culture of this organisation. I have a Masters' degree in psychology, so I am already converted to the idea, but it is still confusing to be faced with the variety of tests on the marketplace. It is a question of trial and error, and deciding which suits your needs best."

A user of psychological testing (public sector executive search firm)

This user has been working in the executive search business for more than 20 years, and in this time his attitude to psychological tests has changed dramatically. He uses a number of tried and tested instruments available on the market, such as OPQ, Belbin and Myers Briggs.

"I find that many of the most popular personality tests are full of Americanisms, which tend to put off my candidates. For example, lots of them don't know what 'pep' is, or who 'sophomores' are.

"It is important to us that our candidates are happy about doing our tests. For this reason, we don't give people too many tests or ones which are too long or tedious. I feel that long sessions of tests are counter-productive. Many more people are being tested nowadays, and will accept doing short tests, especially those with a high degree of face validity.

"We have found that if candidates are asked to spend a whole day being tested, they place too much weight on the results of those tests. It makes them anxious, because they think that the outcome of the entire selection process will depend upon it. It is logical for them to reason that if a whole day is spent on testing, and half a day on an interview, then the testing must be more important than the interview. Tests have become longer and longer as different testing companies try to sell more sophisticated products. Many of the users, both employers and executive search consultants, cannot judge which are the most appropriate tests, and are often quite attracted to these very long and complex instruments. I used to favour them myself, but not anymore.

"We spend a total of between two and a half and three hours on testing our candidates, on average. Typically, we would give people the latest OPQ, which takes between 30 and 40 minutes; and then we would carry out a series of ability tests, related to the job in question. We would use SHL's numeracy, verbal and abstract reasoning tests and then spend about half of the testing time on personality tests.

"I recently heard of complaints by a number of candidates who were being put through tests of between three and six hours, and there have been instances when an entire field of candidates have walked out and refused to undertake the tests they have been asked to do. Inevitably, there will be other instances of this, and this will put pressure on users to have shorter tests for selection purposes. Career development is another issue, and for this purpose some of the longer tests are highly relevant.

"I am very concerned that many employers place too much emphasis on the results of tests, which effectively lets them off the hook in making selection decisions. When the candidates are aware of this, it can make them quite neurotic about how to answer the tests.

"What is the employer looking for? It is particularly worrying for people who have never done a test before. I always ask candidates I am testing if they have done personality tests before. If they haven't, I will give them the opportunity to do a fairly standard test, such as OPQ, as a dummy run. This helps them to be familiar with the test process and takes away the disadvantage which they may face in competition with other candidates. If someone has never done a test before, to be suddenly confronted by about three hours of tests can be quite daunting and can affect their performance so we try to give all our candidates a level playing field.

"We use various tests for recruitment, and we look at a person's Belbin team type which we can get from the OPQ. We use personality tests of some kind for practically every appointment we handle in local government. We see that test results are useful, as they are one more set of information and we use them at the sifting stage, before the candidate goes to the client. Many of our candidates will do half a day with the client later, so we don't overdo it with tests that are too long and involved at this stage.

"Why are we so keen about personality tests? When senior executives fail to make a success of a senior appointment, it is nearly always due to a clash of personality. We make our own appraisal of the personality of the client and the needs of the job, so we can make an appraisal of the personality of candidates which complement them. I find that it is vital to fit the ethos of people to the ethos of the organisation.

"Although many of the clients subsequently test people, I insist on my own tests. In the public sector, it is easier to be quite open in the process of selection. We have to be totally confident that they can do the job, but also we must be sure that their personality will fit the organisation. So even when clients don't want to use testing, we always insist upon it and then play quite a dynamic part in the testing process.

"Some of our clients are concerned that our tests are culturally biased, but we don't believe that this is so. For example, we are looking for people who are naturally gregarious and outgoing, independent and individual, and our tests are normed against populations like this. However, we do realise that we are living in an increasingly culturally-diverse world, and we take this into account. Some of our clients also think that we do things in a rather mysterious way, but we explain to them exactly what is happening, as we do to our candidates.

"However, we don't give feedback to the candidates until after the appointment has been made. We feel that if they know their test results and they are still within the selection process, they may modify their behaviour to offset some of the results of the tests. Doing this may not be in their best interests. We want our candidates just to be themselves and not try to be something different. If a candidate got the job on the basis of modifying their behaviour clearly they would have to carry on permanently modifying their behaviour, which might be a strain. It would be completely dishonest to try to get a job on the basis of false representation of your personality, and you would then have to sustain it, and end up living a lie.

"In over four years, only one candidate has withdrawn from a test, but some people may decide not to put themselves forward in the first place because they don't like the idea of doing tests. It is very important how candidates are treated and they must realise that a test is reasonable and worth doing and should not think the whole basis of the selection decision will be made on the results of the test."

A user of psychological testing (an international executive recruitment firm)

This user has considerable experience of psychological assessment in selection, and hires various psychologists to help with her recruitment needs on behalf of her clients, mostly multinational companies. She is particularly interested in combinations of tests for certain uses. She points to certain problems experienced in her use of testing services, particularly those psychologists who try to do her job for her. She discusses a number of tests below, including the OPQ, 16PF, PAPI, and Belbin.

"I use psychological testing extensively on behalf of my clients in my executive search practice. I find that OPQ is a good off-the-shelf test, but with the important proviso that it's only as good as the psychologist who is administering it and providing the feedback. This can vary enormously, and it's hard to know whom to trust. I have found that, sometimes, psychologists are not content just to test the person and produce the results. Instead, they want to know all about the job the candidates are up for, and they want to make their own comments as to who is suitable. But this is my job, and they're not qualified in appraising and selecting people, and presenting them to the client. They often try to put their own perspectives on the person, and try and match them against a specific job but quite frankly, I don't need this; I just want a professional psychologist who will handle the testing exercise for me. The whole thing hangs on how good a psychologist is at explaining a subjective interpretation. We don't want psychologists trying to be headhunters too!

"I always favour tests of people working in groups, because it is inappropriate to only test people as individuals. In these scenarios, including a psychologist and observers, it is possible to see which of the individuals participating will take the lead, which is the hunter, which is the trouble-maker, and which of the people talk first and think second, and vice versa. People definitely behave differently in groups. The Belbin Team Roles exercise is certainly more relevant than many other tests in this regard.

"The 16PF, the Myers Briggs and OPQ have emerged as favourites for general testing purposes, but one hiccup is now emerging: it has now got to the point where too many people have done them before so there is a constant need to produce new versions, which clearly keeps the psychologists in business. The corollary of this is that the person who has not done such tests before can be at a big disadvantage, and should find out about the various tests available, and gain opportunities to practice.

"The Belbin team role model is good, and this starts people thinking about themselves and their colleagues in group situations. Too many tests are simply geared toward testing individuals in isolation. A test which is only comprehensible to another psychologist is not of much use.

"The PAPI test is very popular with people who have done it, and received the feedback. They like it, and want to use it as a tool in the selection process. Both PAPI and OPQ are good within batteries of tests. They provide a good foundation from which to look at testing other qualities and attributes. Few tests are good enough to be used on their own and, of course, no test or tests can take the place of good structured interviews by a real professional."

Testers' perspectives

A testing company using psychological testing (an audit/assessment firm)

This firm is licensed to offer the DMT, OPQ, FIRO-B, Thomas-Kilmann Mode of Conflict Instrument, Watson's and Raven's and the Bortner Type A Questionnaire.

"There are important ethical questions about assessment techniques. When a company takes someone on, they clearly want to know about him or her, and need to be aware of the particular managerial skills and qualities of each individual on the payroll. Consequently, they need to be able to use a range of tests to reveal these skills and qualities in an accurate and meaningful way.

"However, we believe that it is not necessarily ethical for a company to subject employees to clinical-type tests which analyse their past emotional development from their childhood to the present. Most occupational tests have been developed to explore surface traits, and basic personality types can be revealed without the use of clinical tests. There could be a debate here that more clinical tests, such as the DMT (although widely used in an occupational setting), have little relevance in a job situation. Others may disagree, but we would not want to use this type of test ourselves. We specialise in shorter tests geared very much for the occupational setting, and choose combinations of tests designed specifically for our clients.

"We favour the basic psychometric tests, which are quick to do and quick to score, and which have a published validity. These are quite distinct from the clinical tests, which are conceptually totally different. These quick instruments are, arguably, more important and relevant in the job setting than the longer, more complex assessments. For example, the short Bortner Type A Questionnaire can offer some very useful, quick insights, laying the foundations for further tests.

"We select from tests available, and use a blend of different instruments, put together as a test battery. The aim is to make an objective assessment of surface traits rather than an in-depth clinical analysis.

"In terms of the popular OPQ test, we have developed our own norm, representing a more senior managerial and professional group than the standard SHL norm. The OPQ is a very successful test, but those being tested need to be normed against the most relevant group for maximum accuracy and benefit.

"We have discovered and utilised a range of American instruments which enable the company to offer useful batteries of occupational-related tests. These include the Thomas-Kilmann Modes of Conflict Instrument. We have found these tests to be relevant, revealing and highly appropriate to the needs of our clients and are quite surprised that few other assessment organisations in the UK offer them. None of these tests takes very long to do, but each looks at people from a different perspective. Together, they can provide a very detailed insight into the psychological profile of an individual at work. Singly they may appear limited and slightly esoteric, but together they are powerful and convincing. We are also not wedded to one set of instruments, but we make a selection according to the needs of the client. We are also critical of testing which offers inadequate follow up, as this frustrates testees and makes employers appear unprofessional. Some testees think they have "failed" a job interview through "failing" the psychological test when they don't receive proper feedback.

"In the USA there is considerable legislation and regulation of test usage, but in the UK, testing activities are generally under-regulated, and, arguably, there could be some restriction of this activity. Psychological tests are fundamentally discriminatory, if only in terms of the effect upon people who have not done tests before. The Post Office did a study on test practice and the effect on test results of experience in having done tests generally. People who are familiar with tests tend to take them in their stride much more easily than those who have not done them before.

"We also arrange ability tests, including ability and abstract reasoning tests. The abstract test is especially relevant for senior executives who need to have an ability to think strategically.

"We believe that tests should not be used to make judgements on people as being employable or not employable. Instead, we argue that people are assets, and we need to understand the best way to use them both as a leader and as a subordinate, and also as a member of a team. Our added value comes from our choice of tests to suggest for particular applications, detailed feedback to each person being tested, and relevance of the test to the person, in helping them to the best advantage in a particular environment. Unfortunately, many tests are used in the UK as a substitute for interviewers' judgement, rather than as an adjunct, to help remove responsibility from the personnel people who are trying to avoid it.

"Yet, there are many elements in selection and career development which cannot be satisfactorily tested, such as 'Do you like your job?', 'Will you like a move to another job?', 'Is your job socially acceptable to you?' Many personnel people accused of poor recruiting will blame the tests which are traditionally used in their departments, when they are, in fact, using the tests entirely in the wrong way. The more superficial tests give personnel managers a false sense of security, and there will be a backlash against their use in the near future.

"It is important to talk to users of tests, to look at the numbers of companies and recruiters who use testing as an important step in recruiting. Which people interviewed well but were rejected on their test results? Are people offered jobs on the basis of their test results being accepted, even if their interview was less successful? Does everyone get individual and confidential feedback after each test? Or, do they just get a rejection letter from the potential employer? Are there cases of people spending a whole day completing a variety of psychological tests who then hear nothing more about them? Everyone should receive feedback so that they can have the benefit of having done the test, even if they don't get the job or the promotion.

"We have developed a number of batteries of tests and assessment combinations, and over the course of several years we have found these forms of assessment to be particularly valuable. Watson's and Raven's are used quite widely as ability tests, but we tend to use them to test abstract thinking in senior executives. They are particularly valuable in selecting people for top jobs, used in both job selection, and in career development and succession planning.

"We have found the DMT to be particularly revealing and the results of different candidates for one job can be startlingly different. The DMT provides real insight into psychological make up, and can reveal deep-seated traits which would be missed by the standard occupational tests. Personally, I never cease to be amazed by what it shows but it is not for the mass market. We gear this for senior executives only. These tests deserve to be taken very seriously indeed. They have been developed over a long period of time and have considerable norm groups."

Testees' perspectives

A variety of testees, most of whom had taken a range of test over the years, were asked to talk about each of the ones included in this book. Some opinions were positive, some negative, but all bring up interesting points. When you do the test yourself, you may agree with these perspectives or you may feel differently.

PAPI

"I thought that this was quite a fun test to do, but it was difficult to choose between the statements. I often thought that both of them were irrelevant and inappropriate, and it annoyed me to say that one thing was true of me when I thought it wasn't, although it was more acceptable than the other alternative. I like the wheel design used in the feedback, and the easy to understand summary of the findings. It did match my personality and tendencies at work quite accurately, although some were rather exaggerated. Altogether, it was well worth doing, but it did tend to whet my appetite for more, rather than answer all the questions I had in mind."

Myers Briggs Type Indicator

"This is one of my all time favourites. The personality types are very well thought-out and are good summaries of basic outlook. Yet I have heard that this test can be used to make sure that everyone in a certain organisation is of the same type, and many testees don't like this. The test itself has quite an American style, but is fairly international in application. The test seems to be pretty accurate, because I made a guess of the type I thought I was before doing the test, and came out as I expected."

16PF

"I didn't think that this was quite as straightforward as the Myers Briggs. Some of the questions seemed rather inappropriate and it also seemed a bit old-fashioned. I wasn't that convinced about the feedback as it seemed a bit extreme in the results. Some of the test seemed a bit childish, and the statements rather glib. I think I would have preferred to choose between just two statements, rather than have an in-between option too. But I can imagine that many would find it useful."

OPQ

"I did this test online and it was very efficiently administered. There is an advantage doing it this way: you don't feel you're being tested by a person, but by a machine. The analysis booklet seemed rather cold and formal, and did not reflect the findings as well as a good psychologist could, I'm sure. However, it is quick to score this way, and 10 minutes after finishing the test I was presented with an impressive booklet. The OPQ does give you a huge amount of insight about yourself and it is then just a question of how you interpret it."

FIRO-B

"This test did not seem so geared towards the work setting as many others. The questions seemed to be mostly about your relationships with people, more at home and socially than at work, although I can see that it does have occupational uses, and can be focused on just the workplace. It was relatively easy to do, and quite good in showing how independent and/or sociable you are. It certainly showed another dimension to my personality compared with other tests. I would have thought that it wouldn't be a huge amount of use on its own, but best combined with other, more job-oriented assessments."

Thomas-Kilmann Mode of Conflict Instrument

"This was particularly fascinating and excellent in terms of how you deal with conflict. I had never thought that there were so many different ways of dealing with situations of conflict. It was certainly helpful in terms of the way I saw my role in teams and would be very useful in selecting people for negotiating assignments as how you deal with conflict is a very important part of your daily life at work."

Raven's Progressive Matrices

"These were difficult puzzles, designed to see how well you could spot relationships and make logical deductions. It was a bit like going back to school, and reminded me of abstract exams I did as a child. The real value of these was explained in the feedback as they showed your conceptual thinking, and confidence in making judgements."

Watson Glaser Critical Thinking Appraisal

"This test really made you think and really stretched the mind. There was a lot to read, and a lot to take in and reason out before you could decide on the answers. I can see why this test is used for high-level selection as it is excellent in terms of looking at how, and how well, you think things out. But would you be able to do it more than once? Would it still be valuable then?"

The DMT

"This test changed the whole way I think about myself. I had no idea that my childhood had such an important impact on my current way of thinking. I had never thought about what drives me before, and where my attitudes to work and authority come from. Doing the test is a very strange experience and I found myself talking about it for weeks afterwards. It certainly helps you to discover the make up of your personality. It was almost uncanny in terms of accuracy and insights. I would defy anybody not to be moved by this. But having said all this, the DMT is not necessarily clearly related to your job, unless this is clearly explained in the feedback."

Belbin's Team Roles

"This was the most fun, and most difficult, of all the tests I've ever done, or ever heard of anyone doing. It was also the longest, involving having a couple of days off work because it was used as part of a team-building session, and obviously not everyone could spare this amount of time. But it was really amazing to enact this special game to analyse how different team types behave. I certainly learned a lot about how some teams work well, and why others are chaotic or never produce results. However, I can't see how a company could implement the findings. They couldn't break up all the existing teams and regroup them on the basis of the Belbin types, as certain teams do certain things and need certain people in them regardless of their team type. However, it does help you to be more tolerant of the weaknesses of those you work with."

A professional, academic psychologist's perspective

This professional, academic psychologist has experienced the world of psychological testing throughout his career: as a postgraduate student of Occupational Psychology, as an employer, as a consultant guiding clients on test usage, in counselling candidates on their test results and also in going through a selection procedure himself for each successive appointment in his own career as a management consultant. The use of psychological testing continues to be an area of key concern in his current work, in training and developing management consultants, and in providing coaching and mentoring to management consultants and their senior executive clients. As he comments:

"All the tests mentioned in this book have their applications and value, but no test should ever be used in isolation when making a selection or career progression decision. They are tools to aid human resource decision-making, not a substitute for experienced judgement. Ideally, tests should provide insights into how the candidate might perform and respond to different situations for the purposes of job-matching, counselling and career planning. All tests should be prefaced with the necessary preliminary and explanatory information, and administered in neutral, non-threatening surroundings. The purpose and context of the test should be clearly understood from the outset.

"Psychological tests are a useful adjunct to the vital management job of assessment and selection, which is primarily an information-gathering function. This information should be derived from a variety of sources to build up a comprehensive picture of the individual. Psychological tests are one source, while others include bio-data and personal interviews. A systematic approach to human resource selection and development requires multiple inputs, of which psychological testing is just one.

"Feedback is essential. Administering a test without offering feedback to the candidate is just as incomplete as a test without interpretation of results for the user would be, and is bad professional practice. Using psychological tests without contextual explanation or interactive feedback at best creates bad public relations for the company; at worst, it may even impose lasting damage on an individual, especially if the individual believes – usually incorrectly – that he or she is being denied a job appointment or career progression as a result of 'failing' a test.

"I feel that companies administering tests without appropriate preliminaries and follow-up should lose their licenses or have them endorsed until they demonstrate good practice. Best practice is that candidates should have access to, or vetting rights over, test results, rather in keeping with the sort of safeguards available under the data protection provisions.

"The world of psychological testing has been fraught with controversy from its earliest days. One debate is concerned with the use of traditional, well-validated tests, over newer forms of testing. Many professional psychologists criticise the newer tests as being unreliable or invalid or both, and almost certainly gimmicky. However, many of the newer tests appeal widely to both users and candidates. They can appear modern and relevant, as well as being more appropriate to the modern working environment.

"A further debate – among users rather than psychologists – concerns the face validity, or user-friendliness, of tests generally. There can be an irritability factor with some tests, in which it is hard to see what quality or perception is being tested, and why. Academic psychologists may criticise their applied psychologist colleagues for drifting away from the purity of controlled research and getting their hands dirty in the commercial marketplace, but I am a firm believer in the value of applied occupational psychology, and the traditions of 'fitting the job to the person, and the person to the job'."

A note on computer-based and online testing – how can accuracy be ensured?

With the advent of the internet in psychological testing, many psychologists, users and testees were concerned with the increased possibility of cheating and piracy, especially in ability testing. SHL, one of the largest and most well-established testing companies in the UK, has tried to address this issue with the 'Verify Range of Ability Tests', presented as a solution to online ability testing.

This range of tests is offered by SHL as a solution to unsupervised online ability testing. One of the greatest concerns here is with cheating, and with content piracy aiming to support cheating, to allow a person to gain an inflated score to help in gaining a job offer or promotion, etc. This score might be significantly higher that the person's true ability – and meanwhile the job candidates who have taken the test honestly, but who have gained a lower score than the cheats, could be disadvantaged. Yet using the internet for ability testing is cheap and convenient – organising a test administrator to be present is expensive and difficult, with candidates having to attend a test centre and administrators having to travel and be paid. So this psychological testing company has tried to create home-based yet cheat-resistant tests, which can be followed-up by supervised psychometric verification tests that can be used to validate (or confirm or challenge) the first score.

SHL's Verify range includes Verify Ability Tests – specifically designed for unsupervised administration online – and Verify Verification Tests – which are used under supervision for short-listed applicants. These check the consistency of the scores obtained on these unsupervised tests, flagging inconsistent scores for subsequent follow-up. The unsupervised tests have been created by drawing sets of items from a large bank of questions, such that everyone gets a different but equivalent test. This prevents candidates from finding answer keys to tests, and makes it impossible for candidates to collude by trying to swap answers. The ability tests offered test verbal, numerical and inductive reasoning abilities, at a range of different ability levels. The unsupervised tests provide a final score on each candidate, and the verification test then comes up with a verification result – a simple verified or not verified classification. This takes extra time, obviously – the SHL Verbal Ability Test, with 30 items, takes around 19 minutes to complete, then the Verification Test looks at the answers to 18 items, taking 11 minutes to check consistency. The Numerical Test, with 18 items, takes 25 minutes to finish, then 15 minutes to verify the answers to 10 items. The verification process can be carried out by the user in a variety of different ways to suit each tester.

'Verification' is the process of checking the test to highlight possible inconsistencies which could suggest outside help gained by a candidate. This is not the same as authentication, which is confirming identity, a different but also necessary process. Verification testing is combined with identity-checking of short-listed candidates, and SHL also uses 'data-forensic' analysis methods to check that test questions have not been compromised by over-exposure.

Test users are strongly recommended to use a variety of tests when considering candidates – such as personality tests, culture-fit assessments, well-structured interviews, and analysis of performance in a scenario/role play organised as part of an assessment centre. Say, for example, a test user, in an organisation recruiting new staff, is implementing unsupervised internet-based testing administered by candidates on themselves at home, in order to screen a number of candidates for jobs, cheaply and efficiently. This sounds good, but what if the candidates are cheating by searching for answers online, calling up smart friends for ideas and suggestions, even asking others to complete the exercises for them? How can the test user in the organisation screen-in the promising candidates and screen-out the cheats? In the past, this process was mostly by gut-instinct, especially during a well-structured in-depth interview by an experienced interviewer. Cross-referencing the information from several assessments might also set warning-bells ringing if the results don't add up. If the candidate gained top marks in a numerical reasoning test, but a check with the CV shows a fail for secondary school mathematics exams, it might look suspicious.

By contrast, the tests and the built-in verification system developed by SHL are trying to add some scientific rigour to this process of cheat-detection. This testing company, in presenting the verbal, numerical and inductive reasoning tests, cites the overwhelming evidence from the scientific research literature that measures of cognitive ability are one of the most consistent predictors of job performance, especially for more complex and demanding job roles. Additionally, these tests are related to, or 'normed' against, four different levels of distinct, specific comparison groups (Managerial/Graduate/Supervisory/Operational) and a variety of industry sectors. So these tests are designed to provide a useful screening mechanism, generating in-depth reports. More recently, clerical-level tests of checking and calculation have been added to the Verify range.

However, the tests alone are not expected to give the full picture. This is where the verification process comes in, looking for consistency. Is the test completed by the candidate at home a valid indicator of his or her ability? Or is the candidate's score aberrant and possibly invalid? Does it look like he or she has tried to improve on nature and reality in order to get the job?

So, what does the test user from the organisation carrying out the recruiting do when faced with an aberrant score? Just drop that candidate like a hot potato and move onto another? Not necessarily...he or she may not be cheating. Instead, the candidate could be asked to sit another test from the same stable, this time supervised, and the consistency exercise repeated. There is a need to check against CV information, and results in other exercises and tests. Discussing aberrant scores with a candidate can be problematic – direct confrontation with accusations of cheating might not work here, producing defensive counter-attacks and even threats of legal action. The feedback must be presented in such a way as to emphasise that the purpose of the discussion is to ensure that the assessment is accurate and valid, and to make sure that the candidate has a fair opportunity to carry on with the screening process.

There could be valid reasons why candidate scores are inconsistent – such as illness, tiredness, distraction and therefore lack of concentration, lack of familiarity with testing (although practice tests are provided), and different moods between different days of taking different tests. Have they been inconsistent before, yet doing the tests as honestly as possible?

Sometimes, explaining the verification system at the start puts off potential cheaters. They may be scared of the effectiveness of large-scale computer simulations, and then the potential employer would be warned off them for ever, and that they might be black-listed across a range of organisations and never get a job. The Orwellian 'Big Brother' fear can have a powerful preventative force. SHL maintain they can detect 97% of cheating using this system, to say nothing of perhaps preventing 50% of cheats in the first place by saying they will verify all answers.

So, what is the view of test users of this system? Do they find it useful, effective and adding value to the process? One insight comes from National Australia Bank, written up as a case study by SHL (see Downloads, below). Here, the bank faced the problem of competing against other prospective employers for Australia's top graduates, where time was of the essence. If there was a delay in NAB making offers to these graduates, they might go elsewhere. The bank wanted to conduct a series of tests, and found that online tests were faster, enabling them to identify and secure talent ahead of the pack. For NAB, this was serious business, as every year they recruited around 200 graduates for positions in HR, accounting, technology, investment banking and wealth management. The graduate recruitment cycle was scheduled for April to June each year, and NAB discovered that if they missed making offers any later than the first week in June, they would miss the best graduates. In 2008, NAB received over 7,000 applications, so the work of screening was intense.

These go-getting and ambitious graduates obviously expected NAB to use state-of-the-art technology in recruiting. In the past, NAB had used standard ability tests, supervised in person to prevent cheating. There was an increasing risk that job candidates would be completing the same test, especially as they were considering a number of job possibilities at the same time. So the process was both time-consuming and potentially inaccurate. Using Verify, NAB was able to speed up the early-stage screening process, without the fear of candidates cheating. The randomised nature of the tests, with a million possible combinations of questions, meant that the tests couldn't be repeated, and that candidates couldn't find these tests on the internet. With Verify as a screening tool, NAB then continued to assess second-round candidates with more tests. Graduates joining NAB confirmed that the speed of the process was essential to their decision to join NAB. If they still relied on in-person testing of standard tests, NAB would find it challenging to attract and sign up the number of graduates needed in such a competitive environment.

Contact details: SHL, www.shl.com, UK@shlgroup.com, 0870 070 800

Downloads: Eugene Burke (2006) The Verify™ Range of Ability Tests. User Guide. SHL Group, plc

SHL's Online Testing Helps NAB Win Race to Secure Top Grads, 2008 Case Study

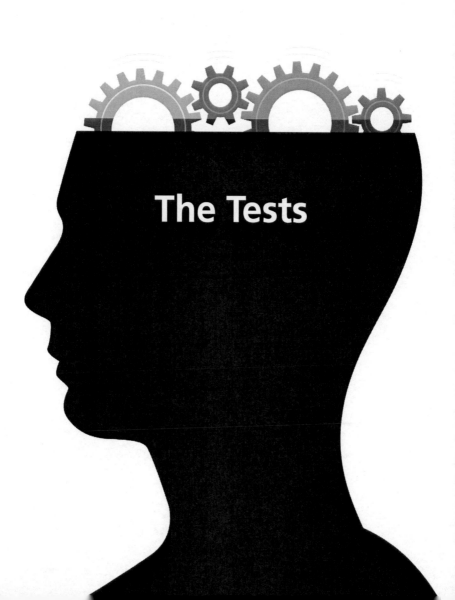

The Tests

Bortner Type A Questionnaire

Background

The Bortner Type A Questionnaire has been chosen as the first psychological test in the book to introduce the subject and help the beginner to experience a soft landing in psychology. People with only a cursory interest in psychology have often heard of Type A and Type B personalities and they are often easily recognisable as types without sitting a psychological test.

The test is a short, easy-to-complete exercise, high on face validity. It can be used as a warm-up exercise to get people used to the idea of being tested. It is often included in batteries of other personality tests, to confirm the trends suggested in other instruments, and to give a rating of the extent to which a person has a Type A personality or Type B personality.

This instrument was originally devised to test people who are likely or unlikely to suffer from heart disease. It was discovered that Type A people were more likely to become coronary patients than Type B people. It was originally developed by Bortner over fifty years ago after analysing hospital patients, and is now used in both clinical and occupational contexts.

The aims of the test

This well-known, simple instrument is used to test the extent to which a person has a Type A or Type B personality. This provides a simple insight for an employer into the people in the organisation who may be subject to stress, i.e. those who are Type A. Some will be higher on the scale than others and, although Type A characteristics are generally prized qualities in an organisation, they can lead to conflict and instability. It can be useful to be able to build teams and groups based on a precise knowledge of employees' personality types.

The format

The test comprises a list of Type A statements listed on the left, and Type B statements listed on the right. The numbers 1-11 are spread across the space between each pair of statements, and the person completing the test simply circles the most appropriate one in each case. There are fourteen pairs of statements in total.

Range of applications

This test is suitable for any selection or management development exercise, and can be used on any person at any level in an organisation. It is extremely general in nature, and is not necessarily occupationally-oriented.

Doing the test

It is simply a case of considering each pair of statements and deciding which is most true about you. If you are positive that the statement to the right – the Type A statement – exactly describes you, then circle 11. If you think it's mostly true, then circle 8 or 9. If the statements on the left more accurately reflect your personality, then you will be choosing numbers 1 or 2, but these will vary. Overall, most people fall clearly into one of the two camps, and it is just a question of the extent to which the statements apply to each individual.

Examples of content of the test

So, what are the differences between Type A people and Type B people? The test lists statements which suggest the following conclusions about Type A and Type B people, and the person completing the test simply decides which are most appropriate in each of the cases:

(Please note. The actual test papers for all tests will have their own visual appearance distinct from the examples throughout the book.)

- Type A people tend never to be late for appointments whereas Type B people are fairly casual about them;
- Type A people are very competitive whereas Type Bs are not;
- Type As often anticipate what others are going to say in conversation, by nodding and attempting to finish the sentence for them, while Type Bs are good listeners;
- Type A people are always rushed and Type B people never feel rushed, even when under pressure;
- Type As are always impatient when they are waiting while Type Bs can usually wait patiently;
- Type As try to do many things at once, and are constantly thinking about what they will do next, while Type Bs take things one at a time;
- Type As are emphatic in speech, and fast and forceful in manner, while Type Bs are slow, deliberate talkers;
- Type As always want to do a good job which will be recognised as such by others, while Type Bs care more about satisfying themselves, no matter what others may think;
- Type As are fast moving in their habits and especially in walking and eating, whereas Type Bs are slow at doing most things;

- Type As are hard-driving in terms of pushing themselves and others, while Type Bs are much more easy-going;
- Type As tend to hide their feelings, whereas Type Bs will express them;
- They As will have few interests outside of their work; whereas Type Bs will have many outside interests;
- Type As tend to be very ambitious and eager to get things done, whereas Type Bs are not ambitious and more casual.

It is fairly simple to define which of these types you are and to what extent, by adding up the scores given against each statement. Taking each of the above variables, simply score yourself from 1 to 11, according to which best reflects the way you behave in your everyday life, particularly at work (here we are looking at the use of this test in an occupational context).

For example, if you are usually on time for appointments (the first pair of statements), you should choose a number between 7 and 11. If you are casual about appointments, you should indicate a number between 1 and 5.

Time needed to complete the test

Only between five and ten minutes, perhaps even less, as the test comprises only fourteen choices. It could take longer if the person answering the test is unsure of the extent to which they are Type A or Type B, as each statement has scale of 11 options. This allows for a central score of six points, with five points on either side, but in practice it is fairly unusual to display a central point.

Time to score the test

This is quickly done, and is just a question of adding up the scores, the number circled against each statement. A Type B person would score between 14 and 84, whereas a Type A person would score between 85 and 154. Scoring a number in the middle between each type – such as 84 or 85 – is quite rare.

Necessary time for feedback

Only about 10 minutes would be required to explain what is a very simple, self-explanatory test, but some of the statements are thought-provoking, and it can be useful to spend some time on these, especially as part of a career development exercise, when this test is used as a basis for discussion of behaviour.

Format/structure of the feedback

In the feedback, you may be asked for practical examples to confirm your choice of scores. If the psychologist or person providing feedback knows you well, he or she will have anticipated your choices. You may be asked which you think are your good or bad characteristics, and why. You may be asked which you think are most helpful in the work context, and those which are not conducive to your success in the organisation. Have any of these qualities resulted in particular problems for you in your work? How do you work with people of the other type? Do they frustrate you (if you are a Type A person), or confuse, tire or baffle you (if you are a Type B person)? Basically, how do you get on with other people, in terms of seeing them as a help or a hindrance.

Value to the employer/user

Most people fall clearly into one of the two types. Type As tend to be more stressed than Type Bs, although it is also a question of how the stress is handled (which is not necessarily shown in the Bortner test). It can be very useful to the employer to know the tendency towards Type A or Type B of staff members, from junior people through to executives, especially in the formation of teams, and in analysing the success of particular individuals working together. Some employers prefer Type As, thinking they will be harder-working or more productive, but the stress generated can work the other way. It depends on the corporate culture (see below).

Value to the employee/person being tested

For a Type A person, this test may help you to realise why you get stressed at times, and you can focus your attention on areas where you can try to offset the effects of this stress. Why are you always rushed? Wouldn't it be possible to leave more time to make appointments and meet deadlines? Why are you always impatient while waiting? Couldn't you accept that sometimes you have to wait, you can't do anything about it, and use the time just to read or think through a problem? Perhaps you should try to eat your meals less quickly, and not rush around the place quite so much. Perhaps you should learn to express your feelings more often, and not keep them bottled up so much? Perhaps you should try to do one thing at a time, and not start something new until you have finished the previous task, and not drive yourself quite so hard. Do others rebel at being pushed quite so much? Try looking at the situation from their point of view. Many who are Type A people would find it useful to develop interests outside of their job, so that they become slightly less obsessed about achieving at all costs.

For Type B people, the test is useful in highlighting areas where they could show more energy and drive. Should they be rather less casual about appointments, and make a greater effort not to be late? Should they take more interest in what others think in terms of their attitudes to tasks, as satisfying themselves may not be enough? Perhaps they should try to speed up their work, to get more done? Type B people tend to have many outside interests from work: are they sure these are not detracting from their commitment to their job? Does their casual nature and approach mean that they are being overlooked for interesting and worthwhile opportunities?

Value to the user organisation

Again, the Bortner Type A Questionnaire is another useful exercise for fitting people into particular organisations, according to their cultures and styles. Some company cultures attract primarily Type

As (such as the macho and work hard/play hard or retail cultures) and some tend to have a large proportion of Type Bs (such as the process and high-risk, slow-feedback cultures). Type As can be attracted to Power cultures, and those which are market-driven and entrepreneurial. Bureaucratic cultures can be acceptable to Type Bs, whilst Type As may find them frustrating. The results of this exercise are also useful in developing individual teams, which need a mix of personality types.

Can the test results be deliberately falsified?

Clearly, if you want to present yourself as a Type A personality and you are something of a Type B (or vice versa) it would be easy to answer the test in a totally different way, but it would soon become obvious in your behaviour and approach if you had falsified the test. This would then reflect badly on your level of personal integrity, which would be damaging to your career. Obviously, the most simple tests are the easiest to falsify, but also attempts to falsify them are the most transparent.

Advantages over other tests

It is simple, quick and gives a clear category rating, useful for both selection and management development exercises, and good as a discussion starter.

Disadvantages compared with other tests

Very simple, not in-depth, could be easily falsified and only shows limited insights. Not complete in itself in terms of giving a picture of an individual.

Tests may be combined with...

This exercise could be combined with more detailed tests, such as the OPQ personality series, as a 'taster' at the start of a series of tests, to help a person to become familiar with test-taking. It could be given to someone who has never attempted a personality test before, to settle them into a long battery of tests over several hours. It could probably be usefully combined with any battery of personality tests, and can be used clinically, as well as occupationally. It could be used with almost any of the tests in this book.

Static/predictive value

It can be very difficult to change your basic personality type, but it may be that the extent to which you are a Type A or Type B could change with change of job or company. Also, Type A's tend to slow down slightly as they get older.

Overall review

Speed of being tested – fast
Speed of scoring results – fast
Cost – low – the test is freely available and out of copyright
Range of applications – wide
In-house/Out-house – either
Basic/Advanced – basic

How to prepare yourself for sitting this test

The test is not intellectually stretching and just requires straightforward and honest answers which reflect your personal characteristics as accurately as possible. You should not worry about right or wrong answers and trying to come over as a specific type; both Type A and Type B people have valuable roles to play in business and in organisations.

Will this test produce a different result after a period of time?

Possibly, as Type A people may become more stressed or less stressed with a change in job, and Type B people may become more laid-back or less. But the basic types are unlikely to change. For Type A personalities who are suffering undue stress, the Bortner Type A Questionnaire could be used after about a year or so, to see if stress reduction has been successful.

Contact details: The Bortner questionnaire is no longer offered commercially and, as more than fifty years have passed since it was first published, it is no longer subject to copyright. Cooper's adaptation of the Bortner Type A scale (date unknown) has been used in this review.

PAPI – The Personality and Preference Inventory

Background

The Personality and Preference Inventory or PAPI is a highly popular work style assessment tool used by more than 1000 employers in over 50 countries. PAPI, devised to form a basis for interview discussions, was designed by Dr Max Kostick, working in the State College of Boston, Massachusetts in the 1960s. It was first used by the management consultancy PA Consulting Group in 1966. PA gained the exclusive worldwide rights to market this questionnaire in 1979, and many employers used it directly under license from PA. PA also offered training courses to instruct license-holders in the most effective use of PAPI. In 2000, PA's Assessment and Development division was formed into a venture company called Cubiks, and in 2004 the Cubiks management team and employees agreed a buy-out from PA. PAPI is now available in over 25 languages and is owned, developed and marketed by Cubiks (see contact details at the end of this section).

The aims of the test

PAPI is probably most useful as a mechanism for structuring an occupational discussion, whether for selection, as part of a team-building exercise, or for personal development and career planning purposes. It is a specifically work-related assessment. As such, it does not seek to answer every question about an individual's inherent personality, but it is useful for opening up discussions around the preferred work style of the respondent.

PAPI has been devised to reveal the nature of an individual's preferred ways of working, and thus how they can be most effectively accommodated in an organisation. Following a discussion based on PAPI, the individual's typical working behaviours can be identified. The assessment indicates how an individual is likely to react in a given work or team situation, plus a range of other areas.

The format

PAPI is short, simple and user-friendly. It is available in two formats: PAPI-I (Ipsative) adopts a forced choice format and requires the respondent to select their preferences from 90 pairs of statements. PAPI-N (Normative) asks the person completing the questionnaire to rate the extent to which they agree with 126 statements. This version of the questionnaire allows employers to compare participants and is made available with an extensive series of norm groups for benchmarking purposes.

Cubiks describes PAPI as 'intuitive, truly work-related and extremely versatile'. As with most of the personality-based tests in this book, there are no rights and wrongs; it is either a question of choosing between two phrases (in the case of PAPI-I) or indicating the extent to which you agree with a statement (PAPI-N) in a fairly instinctive way rather than after long deliberation.

Range of applications

PAPI is typically used for assessing people in graduate and management level roles, for both recruitment and for development purposes. It can be conducted again after time in order to assess changing work patterns and preferences during the respondent's career.

Doing the test

Both questionnaires are delivered online via the Cubiks Online platform. Respondents log in to the platform using a unique log-in code, enter their bio-data, select the language that they would like to complete the questionnaire in and then view a series of short instruction screens and sample questions that help them to understand the nature of the assessment. Once they have completed these steps, they begin the questionnaire.

When completing PAPI-N, the respondent is required to choose the option that best reflects the degree to which the statement describes how they are at work. One statement is presented per screen, followed by seven response options with radio buttons. The options range from 'Absolutely Disagree' to 'Absolutely Agree'.

When completing PAPI-I, the respondent is presented with 90 pairs of statements. They must choose the statement in each pair which most closely describes how they behave at work. There will be pairs of statements where it is difficult to make a choice, but the individual must nevertheless choose one. Each pair of statements should be judged independently, without bearing in mind how previous pairs of statements have been dealt with.

PAPI, like many other assessment tools, deliberately repeats statements to ensure that undue weighting is not given to the way that the respondent reacts to a single specific question. By designing the questionnaire in this way, the developers are able to ensure the tool measures the respondent's working style in a reliable and accurate way, though this can have the effect of it appearing puzzling to some participants.

In the case of PAPI–I, individuals will sometimes find it very hard to choose between the answer options. That they are forced to choose is significant, and the result of making these choices over 90 statements produces the end picture.

The pairs of statements displayed in the PAPI-I questionnaire have been balanced, based on the developers' research, to be equally desirable (or in some cases equally undesirable) things for employees to say about themselves. The questionnaire is forcing the person to state their preferred style. Their preferences may indicate, for example, the kinds of behaviours they gravitate towards when under time pressure.

As with other psychometric instruments, it is important for the respondent to answer the questionnaire honestly, and not to be guided by feedback already received from other tests they have done.

PAPI is a tool that has been designed to provide international organisations with a common assessment language. As such the text avoids country-specific terms/phrases and detailed studies have taken place to ensure the content of the questionnaire items is not biased towards or against any particular country or culture.

PAPI is not designed to be intellectually stretching, although it may tax your decision-making powers. In the case of PAPI-I, respondents may feel that the limited response options do not allow them to provide an accurate representation of themselves. However, when PAPI is interpreted, they are usually satisfied that their preferences have been pinpointed with a large degree of insight, and the discussion will always allow context and subtleties to be highlighted.

Examples of content of the test

For PAPI-N, the person is asked to choose the option that reflects the degree to which the statement describes how they are at work. For example:

Statement: I always work very hard.

Response options:

- Absolutely disagree
- Greatly disagree
- Slightly disagree
- Neither agree nor disagree
- Slightly disagree
- Greatly agree
- Absolutely agree

For PAPI-I, the person is presented with pairs of statements and asked to indicate which best describes them. For example: 'I always want to work very hard' or 'I always keep my emotions under control'; 'I never feel that my best is good enough' or 'I must stay with the job until it is completely finished'; 'I like to show people how to do things' or 'I want to be the best in everything I do'.

Time needed to complete the test

The PAPI test can take as long as 20 minutes, or as little as 10 minutes, depending on the respondent. Either way, this is one of the shortest questionnaires of its kind available. Longer times may reflect a nervousness that the 'right' responses are being chosen, but individuals are encouraged to respond quickly to the statements without becoming too analytical about the exercise.

Time to score the test

PAPI is scored automatically and immediately via the Cubiks Online system. Users are encouraged to invest some time reviewing the respondent's profile (which again is automatically generated by the Cubiks Online system) before the feedback discussion takes place. If the questionnaire is completed in the employer's office as part of a structured assessment process, the discussion will typically take place shortly after the questionnaire is completed. If the respondent completes the assessment remotely, the feedback discussion will usually take place a few days afterwards, although employers are encouraged to not allow too long a gap between test-taking and test-feedback.

Necessary time for feedback

Feedback is an integral part of PAPI and is essential in all cases. It can be as short as half an hour, but this only allows time to scratch the surface of the findings. It is entirely possible to continue for an hour or more, whilst points are clarified and discussion deepens.

The feedback of PAPI is a two-way process and 'ownership' of the results is essential – respondents are encouraged to consider whether the personality profile provides a true reflection of their preferred working style. The interviewer will use the feedback discussion to verify the respondent's profile and elicit information that will be used to support a selection decision or guide personal development planning.

Format/structure of the feedback

PAPI is quick and easy, both to complete and to score, and also to understand in discussion. The results are summarised in a wheel-type design which provides a useful focus for the discussion. Thus, it comes with its own built-in feedback structure, looking at its 20 different factors, seven key areas, 10 needs and 10 roles.

The twenty different factors fit into the seven key areas in the following way.

Seeking to Achieve	Need to achieve Need to be supportive Role of the hard worker
Active Dominance	Need to control others Leadership role
Conscientious Persistence	Organised type Integrative planner Attention to detail Need for rules and supervision
Openness to experience	Need for change Conceptual thinker Need to finish a task
Sociability	Need to relate closely to individuals Need to belong to groups Social harmoniser Need to be noticed
Work Tempo	Ease in decision–making Work pace
Agreeableness	Need to be forceful Emotional restraint

Using the Cubiks Online system, PAPI licence holders are able to generate a wide range of candidate profile reports, interview guides and personal feedback reports that are tailored according to the personality profile of the respondent. Bespoke reports and competency-based interview guides can also be configured to link to an organisation's competency framework or particular job profile. The standard reports available include:

- Report for Managers and Recruiters
- Narrative report for trained users
- Respondent feedback report
- Job Profile Interview Guide
- Coaching Report
- Motivators and Demotivators Report

Value to the employer/user

PAPI has become one of the most popular of the quick-to-administer instruments on the market, used by thousands of employers and completed by millions of employees/job candidates over the last 45 years and more. PAPI is extensively used as a selection and development tool, but can be useful in a variety of other settings too. It gets the ball rolling in starting off a dialogue, and helps people to open up in interview situations.

Value to the employee/person being tested

PAPI is a good introduction to the world of psychological assessments: from the point of view of the person being assessed, the format may appear perplexing while the inventory is being completed, but there is a straightforward, insightful and highly rational end result. It also provides the individual with an opportunity to discuss their preferences at work, and to enter into the assessment process themselves, rather than just leaving the judgement to the assessor.

Value to the user organisation

PAPI can be used to help fit people into organisational structures and styles, according to their work direction, temperament, work style and social nature. An individual's preferred style of working can be determined, and then the issue of how they would fit into the organisation can be considered. PAPI could also be used with implications for training, such as a training needs analysis tool. It is possible to assess an individual's fit with a particular organisational culture, especially if staff members successful in this culture had been profiled, and these profiles were matched with new recruits.

Can the test results be deliberately falsified?

As PAPI is an assessment of personality that does not contain right or wrong answers, is not used with any pass/fail marks, and is designed to form the basis of a discussion with the respondent, there would be limited benefits for individuals who seek to falsify their results. The forced choice nature of the PAPI-I questionnaire, which carefully balances pairs of statements that are deemed to be equally desirable, makes the assessment particularly difficult to fake.

Advantages over other tests

Quicker and easier than many, with a simple and attractive feedback chart and extensive range of feedback reports that are clear and understandable to those unfamiliar with psychological tests generally.

Disadvantages compared with other tests

The deliberate repetition of questions might frustrate some participants and the test may appear rather simplistic to purists.

Tests may be combined with...

PAPI can be used alone or can be combined with other instruments to provide a fuller assessment, such as Myers Briggs and 16PF or Cubiks' own CIPQ instrument (Cubiks In-depth Personality Questionnaire), which may give data on the respondent's underlying personality, thus adding to their view of their preferred work style which the PAPI test reveals.

Static/predictive value

PAPI gives a clear view of the way a person currently operates, and is useful for structuring an interview to gather data to predict how he or she will behave in a specific occupational setting.

Overall review

Speed of being tested – fast
Speed of scoring results – fast
Cost – low
Range of applications – wide
In-house/Out-house – in-house under license or out-house at Cubiks
Basic/Advanced – basic

How to prepare yourself for sitting this test

If you are asked to complete a PAPI questionnaire, you will be provided with detailed instructions and example questions when you log-in to the Cubiks Online system. For PAPI-I, you must choose between pairs of statements throughout the questionnaire, even if this seems difficult, as you would like to choose both or neither! For, PAPI-N, you must indicate the extent to which the statement describes you. In both formats, the statements are simple, straightforward and unambiguous. You should keep an open mind, even if some of the statements appear baffling. It can be best to answer the points fairly quickly and efficiently, without spending too much time on each. Often the first instinct is the most revealing. It can take longer if there is any confusion over what a certain statement means.

Will this test produce a different result after a period of time?

It may do, as it reflects changing needs and working experiences. It would need to be repeated after a year to two years, especially during career change situations.

Contact details: Cubiks, www.cubiks.com, tel. 01483 544200

Downloads: PAPI brochure; PAPI in Cubiks Online brochure, Interview Guides brochure

MBTI or Myers Briggs Type Indicator

Background

The Myers Briggs has a long history and is still an increasingly popular personality questionnaire which looks at thinking and relating styles, and ways of taking in information and making decisions; it offers a classification of sixteen personality types. These are based on four different personality constructs, developed on the basis of Jungian psychology, which were identified and developed by three generations of the Briggs family, most recently by Isabel Briggs Myers. They have built on Jung's theories and have succeeded in applying these to the occupational setting.

This famous instrument, which was first available in around 1946 (and the first commercial version in 1975), has now been extremely well validated, with extensive type distribution information available for many comparison groups, and has become a favourite among a wide range of employers. The version reviewed in the first edition of this book, with widespread use both in the USA and the UK, was developed and copyrighted in 1976-7. It is distributed by CPP Inc. of California, and a newer version (the European Step 1, developed for the UK market) is now available through OPP.

The aims of the test

The Myers Briggs Type Indicator aims to classify people accurately according to specific personality types, which are now well respected and widely referred to in a variety of organisations. The questionnaire is based on four bi-polar scales, producing sixteen possible combinations or broad personality types. The categories are based on extroverts and introverts, sensing types and intuitive types, thinking types and feeling types, and judging and perceiving types.

The format

The Myers Briggs instrument (the European Step 1 questionnaire) includes 88 items, is fully anglicised, and includes a) and b) options.

Range of applications

The Myers Briggs is used in career development, team-building, management development and sometimes in selection. It has a wide range of applications as a basic personality questionnaire, and is particularly appropriate at the beginning of a battery of different tests, especially because it is so user-friendly, and even pleasant and enjoyable to complete, certainly more so than many of the other available assessment tools.

Doing the test

In completing the Myers Briggs questionnaire, it is simply a case of answering a series of pairs of statements by choosing either a) or b). The options are not too extreme, and in most cases it is easy to make a choice. The Myers Briggs instrument has been adapted considerably over time and has now been extensively refined to give it increased face validity. Of particular appeal is a section listing words, usually a series of opposites, but these are quite subtle (such as 'foundation' and 'spire', for example).

Examples of content of the test

The testee is asked to choose A or B in each case. They are asked to select the option which most accurately describes their feelings and behaviours. Examples (reproduced here with permission of CPP) include:

> **Are you inclined to**
> A. value sentiment more than logic, or B. logic more than sentiment?
>
> **Do you prefer to**
> A. arrange dates, parties, etc. well in advance, or B. be free to do whatever looks like fun when the time comes?
>
> **Which word in each pair appeals to you more?**
> A. systematic, or B. casual; A. sensible, or B. fascinating?
>
> **Which answer comes closest to describing how you usually feel or act?**
> When you start a big project which is due in a week, do you A. take time to list the separate things to be done and the order of doing them, or B. plunge right in? At parties, do you A. do much of the talking, or B. let others do most of the talking?
>
> **Which word in each pair appeals to you more?**
> A. imaginative, or B. realistic; A. devoted, or B. determined?

Time needed to complete the test

The Myers Briggs Step 1 with 88 items takes about 20-30 minutes to complete.

Time to score the test

Can be quickly scored for the feedback session at the same meeting, especially in the computer-based version, which is immediate.

Necessary time for feedback

Feedback can take around an hour, but this depends on the objectives of the session and can often be longer. There is a lot in a typical Myers Briggs feedback session, and it can also be used to identify the phase in which the individual is currently operating, depending on age and situation. This can be very powerful, helping to explain current attitudes and perceptions.

Format/structure of the feedback

The answers given in the scores reflect the four separate preferences of the Myers Briggs exercise; either extrovert (E) or introvert (I); sensing (S) or intuitive (I); thinking (T) or feeling (F); and judging (J) or perceiving (P). Understanding the differences between these types is fundamental to making the most of this test. Each combination of preferences tends to be characterised by its own set of interests, values and skills, and can be matched to appropriate career choices.

In the feedback session, the person administering the assessment will analyse the subject's scores according to their preference for extroversion/introversion, sensing/intuitive, thinking/feeling, and judging/perceptiveness. Everyone doing this test will have specific preference scores according to their results, and these form the personality type, made up of a combination of four from the letters E, I, S, N, T, F, J, P. Obviously, most test-takers are concerned about what each of these preferences means, and the implications.

The purpose of the instrument is to discover 'best-fit' type, decided upon by the testee themselves. This may or may not be the type first recorded in the results. Being described as an **extrovert** means that you probably relate more easily to the outer world of people and things, than to the inner world of ideas. An **introvert**, on the other hand, is more aware of what is going on inside his or her own mind. Much of this form of analysis is based on Jung's division of people into groups who like action and activity, and those who like their own space.

Much of this issue is a question of where you get your energy and drive from, and what takes away your energy and makes you feel drained. In extreme cases, it is sometimes hard for an extrovert to understand an introvert's form of activity and attitudes, and vice versa.

Then there is the second dimension, described as that of **sensing** compared with **intuition**. People who are sensing prefer to work with known facts rather than look for possibilities and relationships. Those with a high preference for intuition would rather look for possibilities and relationships than work with known facts. Sensing people are practical and handle routine well but by contrast, intuitive people don't like routine, and prefer the world of ideas.

The third scale is **thinking** compared to **feeling**. What do you do when you have gathered your facts and impressions? A thinking person will base their judgements more on impersonal analysis and logic than on personal values, whereas a feeling person will base judgements more on personal values and sentiment.

Finally, the fourth dimension looks at **judging** as opposed to **perceiving**. The judging attitude probably means you like a planned, decided, orderly way of life, more than a flexible and spontaneous way. The opposite of this is a perceptive attitude which probably means you like being adaptable and doing things on the spur of the moment. You are less likely to plan, or make decisions quickly, or follow order. This scale also separates those who value being well organised and structured, from those who thrive on ambiguity.

The Myers Briggs exercise tends to emphasise the positive side of your nature and can be very helpful in understanding your strengths. Many managers tend to be the ESTJ type (extrovert, sensing, thinking, judging), i.e. most of their scores are on the extrovert scale, although they can be also intuitive as well as sensing. (This suggests stereotyping, but this is not necessarily the case, as this is not how Myers Briggs is used; you can be a successful manager and not be one of these types.)

The Myers Briggs Type Indicator provides brief descriptions of each type. But the testee is discouraged from putting themselves in a water-tight box. Sometimes, a testee shows almost equal preferences for opposite tendencies, but each testee can eventually find their true underlying preference.

The MBTI gives detailed feedback on each type. For example, a person who is type ESTJ is described as 'practical, realistic, matter of fact, with a natural head for business. Not interested in subjects they see no use for, but can apply themselves when necessary. Like to organise and run activities, may make good administrators especially if they remember to consider others' feelings and points of view'.

By contrast, the opposite of an ESTJ type would be an INFP, who would be described as 'full of enthusiasms and loyalties, but they seldom talk of these until they know you well. They care about learning, ideas, language and independent projects of their own. They tend to undertake too much then somehow get it done. Friendly, but often too absorbed in what they are doing to be sociable. They tend to be little concerned with possessions or physical surroundings'. However, although these types sound completely different, it is possible that various elements might overlap, but the testee will have clearer preferences for some dimensions than others.

Each of the types are analysed in more detail in a typical feedback session and this is matched to the work scene. For example, we will look in detail at ESTJs, a very popular profile for a manager. Other types are reviewed in equal detail in a typical feedback analysis. ESTJs tend to be logical, analytical, decisive and tough minded, and are able to organise facts and operations well in advance. ESTJs make useful contributions to an organisation, in terms of seeing flaws in advance, being able to critique plans in a logical way, being able to organise the processes, products and people, and also being able to monitor to see if the job is done and able to follow through in a step-by-step way.

The **leadership style** of a typical ESTJ is to seek leadership directly and take charge quickly, apply and adapt past experiences to solve problems, be crisp and direct at getting to the core of the situation, be quick to decide, and act as a traditional leader who respects the hierarchy. ESTJs prefer work environments with hard–working people focused on getting the job done. They are task-oriented, well-organised and structured, and provide stability and predictability. They are focused on efficiency and like to reward the achievement of goals.

The **potential pitfalls** which face the ESTJ include the possibility that they may decide too quickly, they may not see the need for change, they may overlook the niceties involved in working to get the job done, and may be overtaken by their feelings and values if they ignore them for too long. ESTJs should consider all sides before deciding, including the human element, and may need to remind themselves to look at the benefits of change. They may need to make a special effort to show appreciation of others, and may need to take time to reflect and identify their feelings and values.

Value to the employer/user

The Myers Briggs exercise looks in detail at the preferences of an individual, and identifies a particular personality type which can be a focus for discussion in management development, team-building, and occasionally in selection. It can sometimes be difficult for one Myers Briggs type to understand another's viewpoints, so this exercise – called a "type indicator" – can be helpful in team-building, and helping specific types to come to terms with others' strengths and weaknesses.

Some organisations have developed a particular enthusiasm for the Myers Briggs and use it extensively on people coming into their organisation, and in matching people to specific tasks. However, it has been suggested that it should not be used to 'pigeon-hole' people but used in discussions of choice of task. There is almost endless literature about the uses and applications of this test.

Value to the employee/person being tested

It can be very helpful for an individual to explore their own preferences, and become aware of their strengths and their particular development needs. When you understand the different Myers Briggs types, it becomes a very useful way of understanding the personalities of the people around you. It can be possible to guess at it, but we are not always aware of someone's true type. It certainly helps to see yourself in your context more effectively, and to know your strengths and weaknesses in a more readily understandable form than in some of the other basic personality tests.

Value to the user organisation

Myers Briggs types can be readily matched with corporate culture types, and can be mixed and matched in team groups. In some organisations certain 'types' may be more frequently represented in certain roles but it is important to remember that different types can complement each other and stereotyping is to be avoided. It could be said that Es are more suited to market-driven and entrepreneurial cultures, and Is to bureaucracies, but this cannot necessarily be seen as a general rule. Js might be more successful in fast-paced, action-oriented organisations, with Ps in more consultative or counselling roles. It has been suggested that the Sensing and Intuitive, and Judging and Perceiving dimensions, can also give an indication of a fit into an unstructured and ambiguous organisation.

Can the test results be deliberately falsified?

It could be fairly easy to falsify Myers Briggs results, because the intention of the questions can be seen as fairly transparent, which is one of the reasons why this instrument is not recommended by psychologists for testing purposes. Sometimes the basic Myers Briggs questionnaire shows an individual to be close to several types, which can be due to inconsistency in the answers. The most important issue is to use the instrument to discover 'best-fit type', the closest of the range of types to the testee.

The very large army of consultants specialising in the Myers Briggs exercise has developed their own techniques to pinpoint types, and it would be difficult for an individual to try to present themselves as a desired, but not real, type.

Advantages over other tests

The Myers Briggs exercise produces clearly-defined types, and discussion allows subtle differences to be explained, which can be used to analyse most people effectively. It is well respected and particularly user-friendly. It can be very useful in easily comparing yourself to others, such as "I'm an ENTJ, what are you? An ENFP? How interesting!"

Disadvantages compared with other tests

If not used appropriately, Myers Briggs does tend to slot people into one of the sixteen types without much leeway, and clearly people are more different and diverse than this. It requires some sympathy with, and understanding for, the underlying psychology, and not everyone has this and is prepared to study it.

However, it should be emphasised that the Myers Briggs recognises that everyone is different, and the exercise looks at 'preference' rather than a black-and-white, extreme profile. It should not be used categorically to pigeon–hole people, but as an aid in understanding. There should always be discussion about the preference scores and what they mean, especially in a particular workplace.

Tests may be combined with...

The Myers Briggs can be used on its own, but could also be used with other measures to gain a fuller picture. It might be interesting to combine the Myers Briggs with the DMT, to further understand the evolution of a specific character, such as extreme types and their development over time. Myers Briggs could also be combined with Thomas-Kilmann, but the outcome might be more predictable and less interesting. Usage combined with the 16PF and FIRO-B is also common.

Static/predictive value

Myers Briggs provides a useful present picture of the individual, and is indicative of how people are likely to behave in given situations, based on the appropriate personality type. With the four phases of a person's lifespan, this test can also suggest how people will evolve and change over time.

Overall review

Speed of being tested – fast
Speed of scoring results – fast
Cost – low
Range of applications – wide
In-house/Out-house – in-house, under license
Basic/Advanced – basic, although more advanced versions are available, including Type Dynamics and Step II

How to prepare yourself for sitting this test

It should be borne in mind that the Myers Briggs Type Indicator aims to define personality types based on an individual's responses to a series of statements, and includes questions which deal overall with the way you like to use your perception and judgement, i.e.

the way you like to look at things and the way you like to go about deciding things.

It is best just to 'be yourself', and any subtleties which do not come through in the test can be brought up in the discussion. Although many managers are ESTJs – for example – it doesn't mean that you could not be an effective manager if you were a different type.

Will this test produce a different result after a period of time?

This is unlikely, unless you have undergone a total change of career, or if you are still developing your preferences in these areas. You may discover that you have moved from one phase of your profile to another, and your overall type may be more clearly reinforced.

Contact details: OPP, www.opp.eu.com, tel. 0845 603 9958

Downloads: Eugene R. Schnell, Leadership Report using the FIRO-B and MBTI Instruments, Report Presented for Test Case 107102009, Oct 07, 2009 – www.cpp.com
Product fact sheet: MBTI Instrument – MBTI Step I
Product fact sheet: MBTI Instrument – MBTI Step II
Naomi L. Quenk and Jean M. Kummerow – MBTI Step II – Interpretive Report – sample
Allen L. Hammer – MBTI – Career Report – sample
Allen L. Hammer – MBTI – Team Report – sample
Allen L. Hammer – MBTI – Work Styles Report – sample

(See also Further Reading.)

16PF

Background

The 16PF (the 16 personality factors), like the Myers Briggs and many of the other personality tests reviewed in this book, is also a very popular, fairly quick-to-use inventory. The Industrial Society in the UK, in their guide to assessment and selection (see Further Reading, below), rated the 16PF as one of the most highly relevant among the many personality questionnaires which have been successfully developed for use with normal populations, and which have shown promise in personnel selection.

As a model of personality types, the 16PF has rapidly become well accepted in the psychometric field, and is one of the most well-known standard tests. Devised by Cattell from 1946-9, the 16PF is based around the idea that an individual's personality consists of sixteen different personality factors, a conclusion which was also based on the application of factor analysis to statements about the individual's personality. It is still used extensively, and is also available in French, German, Spanish, Croatian, Turkish, Japanese, and Traditional Chinese.

More and more validation studies have been carried out, with a number of normative groups now developed. The large amount of normative data available adds considerably to the value of 16PF. This personality questionnaire, based on the first Cattell model, but considerably refined over the years, has provided a profile of the individual's personality which has given a far more sophisticated picture than the first simple Eysenck model (described in the Introduction) would provide. There are several textbooks and learned treatises on each of these different personality types (see Further Reading).

This test, used prescriptively, looks at combinations of personality types and provides a picture of the individual, combining sixteen unrelated factors.

The aims of the test

The 16PF can be used, among other applications, for identifying personalities which fit specific profiles for occupational applications. For example, it would be possible to identify a sales person profile, a manager profile, a researcher profile and a number of other profiles which can be matched against individuals. There can be some inherent contradictions in 16PF and it may be necessary to carry out extensive further testing to find out what is driving the person, in order to explain the personality type into which they seem to fit most appropriately. The test has been normed extensively over many years.

The format

16PF includes a list of just over a hundred statements, and it is simply a case of choosing between two statements given, with the option also to choose a midway answer. Thus there are three options to each statement, and the testee is asked to choose the first natural answer which comes to mind and not to opt for the in-between option, or perhaps only rarely. This option might be seen by the testee as being neutral and a way of avoiding making difficult decisions.

Range of applications

Mostly used in selection procedures, in middle and senior management, but can be used at other levels. A wide range of reports is available, including a Competency Report, a Practitioner Report, a Profile Report and a Career Development Report, giving an in-depth look at the testee.

Doing the test

This test takes about half an hour to complete, because there are basically more options to choose from, with the three possible answers of yes, in between, and no; true, in between, false; and yes, sometimes, no. The questions are simple and straightforward, and it is relatively easy to choose between them. However, if the testee is familiar with the idea of doing tests with only two options, it is easy for him or her to forget that the third option of 'in between' is available. It is open to dispute as to whether or not the instruction – given at the start of the test – to choose the in-between option no more than every four or five times is a good idea. It might lead to a uniformity of scores as people doing the test seek to follow the rules (or ignore them). Either way it can be distracting to the test-taker.

Examples of content of the test

Typical 16PF statements are shown below, and are to be answered by opting for true, in between, or false. The 16PF also includes a number of logical reasoning tests. There are always three options accompanying every question. They are all of general application and are not work-related, or not apparently so.

Examples of 16PF statements (reproduced here with permission from OPP), with question marks representing the in-between option, are:

---

1. **When I look at my work, I tend to notice all the mistakes and imperfections.**
   a. rarely, b. ?, c. often

2. **When I work on a project I like:**
   a. working alone, b. ?, c. working as part of a team

3. **People describe me as:**
   a. accommodating, b. ?, c. persistent

4. **I often find myself going along with things rather than doing what I prefer.**
   a. often, b. ?, c. rarely

---

5. On television, I usually prefer watching an action movie than a programme about art.
   a. often; b. ?; c. rarely

6. I act:
   a. most often on facts and logic, b. ?, c. most often on sensitive intuition

7. In a room full of strangers, I quickly find a group of people and introduce myself.
   a. rarely, b. ?, c. often

8. When I become the centre of attention during a conversation:
   a. I feel very uncomfortable; b.?; c. I really like it

9. I tend to cope with day-to-day challenges and disappointments.
   a. rarely; b. ?; c. often

10. People describe me as:
    a. impulsive; b?; c. calm

Time needed to complete the test

About 30 minutes.

Time to score the test

About 10-15 minutes on the self-scoring sheet.

Necessary time for feedback

Often about 20-30 minutes, but may vary depending on the objectives of the feedback and the practice of the psychologist concerned. It will also depend on if the 16PF has been used with other tests, which is often the case.

Format/structure of the feedback

In the feedback, the 16PF results are then related specifically to personality characteristics, which have been well-validated, given the long history of this exercise. The 16PF results can be examined in depth to produce a detailed report, or can be used just to create a quick profile. There are also a number of second order factors, which can be looked at in more detail.

The 16PF, as the name suggests, examines personality types according to sixteen personality factors, and is also useful for analysing stress levels and anxiety. The 16PF is not specifically work-related, giving indications of aspects of general personality. Details of the implications of this for the work environment can be explored in the feedback. Some of the descriptions in the 16PF seem rather negative, yet it can be useful in the structuring of an interview, and in looking at reasons for success or failure in a given work situation. This issue of negativity has been substantially addressed in recent years, by redesigning and rewording some of the items, for example. The second order factors can be looked at in more detail, and males and females can be scored slightly differently.

For many testees, this can often be the first psychological test they have encountered.

Value to the employer/user

The 16PF is one of the most well-known tests and has been very popular on a long-term basis with many employers. Some companies use it without other tests and without discussion, which is probably not advisable. The 16PF provides a sound, basic personality description which is of value as a general tool for use in interviews for selection, and sometimes for career development and team-building. It can be useful for comparing one person with other employees for possible selection purposes.

Value to the employee/person being tested

This test provides a useful basic introduction to different personality types for the newcomer to psychology, and is still valuable to those who have been profiled many times. The reports generated can be a very good take-away for job candidates and existing employees. It is recommended that the job candidate insists on receiving such tests results; even if he/she doesn't get the job, at least this profile can prevent the feeling that taking the test was a waste of time, and the insights gained may help in further career choices.

Value to the user organisation

16PF results can be linked to particular corporate cultures, especially relating to the amount of risk required in operating in a certain corporate environment. They can be compared with Belbin and used for team-building, especially when used in combination with OPQ and other more occupationally-oriented tests. Some organisations use 16PF to build up profiles of their more successful staff members.

Can the test results be deliberately falsified?

There is a concern that the 16PF might be easier to falsify than some other personality tests, which could be a problem because it is extensively used in selection. However, the basic personality profile can probably be revealed during the feedback and face-to-face interviews, which would show up any attempts to falsify it.

As with all the tests reviewed in this book, users and employers are asked to consider other ways of assessing candidates, and are warned against relying unduly on one instrument.

Advantages over other tests

The 16PF offers a more in-depth discussion than a number of other basic personality tests, and it is well-established with extensive norm groups, in contrast with some of the newer tests. Although still widely used in this form, many users are considering the 15FQ+ (see below).

Disadvantages compared with other tests

The 16PF is very well established as one of the traditional questionnaires, but – as with other instruments – used incorrectly it can be almost dangerous, and it most certainly needs opportunity for feedback discussion. There are some strict guidelines as to training in the use of 16PF, but these are not always adhered to and it can get diluted in value. To some testees, the 16PF does not appear to have immediate occupational value, because it does not appear to be specifically geared towards the workplace, but to more general personality traits.

Tests may be combined with…

The 16PF may be combined with other personality type indicators, such as the Myers Briggs or OPQ, to gather more in-depth information, or PAPI to look at how the individual's personality can be seen in his or her work style. This could also be combined with the Thomas-Kilmann to assess attitude to conflict.

The Belbin Team Role model was originally formulated using the 16PF, and hence is arguably better assessed using 16PF and 15FQ+. Both of these tests can be used to directly predict the Belbin Team Roles.

Static/predictive value

The 16PF has a good static value of personality profile, and can predict behaviour, also in teams.

Overall review

Speed of being tested – moderate
Speed of scoring results – moderate
Cost – low
Range of applications – especially selection
In-house/Out-house – in-house
Basic/Advanced – basic

How to prepare yourself for sitting this test

The questions are general and easy to complete, to be answered with an entirely open mind, without necessarily thinking of the implications of any of the answers. It is very straightforward and does not need advanced intellectual inputs.

Will this test produce a different result after a period of time?

Possibly, but not often, as the basic personality type revealed by 16PF will not change radically over time.

Contact details: OPP, www.opp.eu.com, tel. 0845 603 9958

Downloads: 16PF Career Development Report – sample, OPP Ltd
16PF Interpretive Report – sample, OPP Ltd
16PF Profile Report – sample, OPP Ltd

15FQ+

Background

The 15FQ+ has been created by Laurence Paltiel (broadly related to the same style of exercise as the famous 16PF exercise, above, but representing a significant update). This relatively newly-developed test has been designed to provide a comprehensive assessment of personality, especially within an international business environment, and is used in many locations – it is available in French, Spanish, Russian, Indonesian, Chinese and Arabic. Maintaining the breadth of the original 16 personality factors, first identified by Raymond Cattell in the 16PF, the 15FQ+ is available in a long (200 item) and short (100 item) form. The test materials have been created to make them easier and quicker to complete, score and profile, than the original 16PF (although this classic test is still in popular use).

The aims of the test

Psytech, a well-known psychometric testing consultancy distributing the 15FQ+, argue that the 15FQ+ measures the same personality factors discovered by Cattell and colleagues over 50 years ago, but with higher reliability and validity than has been possible before. Also, 15FQ+ includes a number of extra criterion measures such as Emotional Intelligence, Team Role, Management and Subordinate Styles, Career Themes and Counter-Productive Work Behaviour. The latest edition of the 15FQ+ measures fifteen of the core personality factors first identified by Cattell in 1946. Psytech suggest that they have produced a shorter but more reliable measure of these primary personality factors.

In addition, the 15FQ+ has been designed to use international 'business' English; to avoid race and gender bias; to be completed in less than 30 minutes; to be scored and profiled in under 10 minutes; to be supported by an expert system generating reports and be available in short form.

The 15FQ+ factors or dimensions being measured in this test, related to the 16PF, can be summarised as:

Distant and aloof / Empathetic	Low / High Intellect
Affected by feelings / Emotionally stable	Accommodating / Dominant
Sober serious / Enthusiastic	Expedient / Conscientious
Retiring / Socially bold	Hard-headed / Tender-minded
Trusting / Suspicious	Concrete / Abstract
Direct / Restrained	Confident / Self-doubting
Conventional / Radical	Group-oriented / Self-sufficient
Informal / Self-disciplined	Composed / Tense-driven

The 15FQ+ also takes into account the 'Big Five' Global Factors of personality:

- Introversion/Extraversion
- Low/High Anxiety
- Pragmatic/Open
- Independence/Agreeableness
- High and Low Self-control

This theoretical foundation helps give more substance to the test.

The format

The test, conducted online, offers 200 true/false or one-way options, suggesting that testees should avoid the middle or neutral answer wherever possible. The opportunity is presented to select an option in each case, with the possibility for the testee of changing his or her mind by selecting another option before submitting the completed test.

Statements are offered for the testee to choose true/false or one option, such as:

> *I prefer to keep a distance from people I do not know well*
>
> *Most people are motivated by self-interest.*
>
> *People say that I can be too hard on myself.*
>
> *I consider my views to be different from those of most people.*
>
> *It is important to show respect towards people of higher status or authority.*
>
> *I am always coming up with new ideas, even if some are impractical.*
>
> *I am careful to avoid saying things that might seem out of place.*
>
> *My mood seldom varies from day to day.*
>
> *I can't stand being on my own for long periods.*
>
> *It is more important to obey the spirit than the letter of most rules.*
>
> *A little risk adds excitement to life.*
>
> *I am prepared to take the blame for something someone else has said or done.*

This style of statement continues over the course of the test, in random order, with no clear impression of the personality dimension being tested.

Range of applications

The outcome of the test can be used for a variety of purposes – the selection process in recruitment, and for training and development. It can be used to deploy fresh graduate employees into different departments, looking at specific aptitudes of individuals and how they might enjoy a job working directly with customers, or in a back-office environment, for example. With its extensive international norms, this test is useful for multinational companies, or businesses wishing to use Western psychometric tools but whose staff are mostly non-Western. There are many examples of this test proving valuable in non-Western environments where other tests have been rejected as too challenging or incomprehensible. The same could be said for the 16PF.

Doing the test

This test was fun and easy to do, although this may just reflect the subjective viewpoint of the reviewer. It was neither frustrating or perplexing, and in most cases it was not difficult to make a choice of the true/false items. The need to choose the middle option because of an inability to decide on the main contrasting items came up very rarely. Somehow the choice between objects and activities, which seemed on the face of it to have nothing to do with personality – such as:

> *I like fast sports cars – or a beautiful sunset.*
>
> *I enjoy watching boxing/ice hockey – or gymnastics/figure skating.*
>
> *I prefer reading a real-life crime story – or an historical/romantic novel.*

– was never difficult, but was highly revealing of personality traits. Overall, this test is not a problem to complete, and the efforts to make it internationally-acceptable are clearly apparent. Testees from Asia, Africa and the Middle East may find this test easier to complete than some of the more 'American' style exercises.

Examples of content of the test

See above – most of the test comprises statements which can be interpreted by the testee as true or false, or presents either/or options.

There is always a middle choice in each of the 200 items but – as explained above – the testee is advised not to choose this "too often".

Time needed to complete the test

Around 25 minutes is recommended, and this is generally enough time. As the designers recommend, it is probably a good idea not to spend too much time pondering each item, but to go through the test instinctively. It is easy to gain momentum and speed through this one.

Time to score the test

The test can be scored in around 10 minutes and a report can be automatically generated.

Necessary time for feedback

This depends on the time available and purposes of using the test, but around 30-45 minutes is usually enough to go through the points of the report.

Format/structure of the feedback

Psytech provides a choice of over a dozen report styles for user and testee feedback. Extended reports include those on team role behaviour, leadership, subordinate styles, career orientation, strengths and development needs. There is also a Job Match profile where a respondent's profile is compared to the ideal for a given role with an 'Interview Prompt Report' providing questions to guide a feedback interview. All the reports, according to Psytech, can be generated using a comprehensive normative base of over 2,000 UK professional people. The report generated during this review looked at validity scales, interpersonal styles, thinking styles, coping styles, Team Roles, Leadership Styles, approach to influencing, career themes – and the strengths and potential development needs of the individual concerned.

Value to the employer/user

Uses here are extensive, especially because of the insights on teamwork and leadership styles, and how an individual might work effectively as a subordinate to another person. A team leader might find this test particularly valuable with a small group of employees, to understand the dynamics of how they might work together most effectively.

Value to the employee/person being tested

This test provides a lot of information in one exercise, so can save time for the job candidate or employee. The insights gained into emotional intelligence, team roles and management and subordinate styles can be very useful. How do I work with other people? This test gives the testee a comprehensive answer to this question, as well as indicating career development themes suggesting future job options.

Value to the user organisation

As mentioned, this test can be useful in making deployment decisions for new employees, especially through the Job Match profile referred to above, and through the insights into career development direction provided. If the whole organisation makes use of this exercise, it can be even more powerful. Profiles can be drawn up of employees in specific job roles and the dimensions can be aligned towards preferred character traits in the organisation.

Can the test results be deliberately falsified?

As in the case of the 16PF, the 15FQ+ might be easier to falsify than some other personality tests, which could be a problem because it is extensively used in selection. This would be difficult as it is not obvious what the test is looking for in many of the true/false or alternatives questions, listed above. There have been cases of testees deliberately selecting the opposite of their first choice, in order to confuse the tester and produce invalid results, but the motivation for doing this would seem to be counter-productive.

Advantages over other tests

Wide-ranging, extensive applications are available from 15FQ+, so in cases where there is not much time to test a large number of candidates, this test could be used on its own and could give detailed insights.

Disadvantages compared with other tests

As in the case of many similar tests, the true/false format might be seen by some to be irritating and restrictive, and the point of the test – the face validity – might be seen as low at times. But the user-friendliness of the test can be seen as an important advantage.

Tests may be combined with…

This test can be used with more Specialist tests, such as the Conflict Mode Instrument, the DMT, the GCAA, Raven's and the Watson Glaser, as a basic test which can form a foundation for further testing activities, perhaps for specific roles. The 15FQ+ is one of the few tests which can be used by itself to produce quite a comprehensive test profile of an individual, without recourse to using several tests.

Static/predictive value

The test should be repeated after a major job change and more experience, but the shelf-life would seem to be at least one–two years. An overseas posting might also change the perception of an individual on some dimensions.

Overall review

Speed of being tested – fast
Speed of scoring results – fast
Cost – moderate to expensive, but offering good value due to range
of applications
Range of applications – wide
In-house/Out-house – through Psytech or Team Focus
Basic/Advanced – moderately basic but with extensive implications
in the results

How to prepare yourself for sitting this test

No preparation is needed, except to be prepared to take an open
mind, and to enjoy this as a fun and stimulating activity with a
useful outcome. It is certainly not a chore to complete this test, so
it should not be interpreted negatively.

Will this test produce a different result after a period of time?

Possibly, but this period of time might be longer than with many
other similar tests, especially because of the wide range of
dimensions tested.

Contact details: Psytech, info@psytech.com; lpaltiel@psytech.com;
tel. 01525 720003; this test is also distributed by Team Focus,
roy.childs@teamfocus.co.uk, tel. 01628 637338

Downloads: The Myths and Realities of Psychometric Testing,
from www.Psytech.co.uk
Fifteen Factor Plus Questionnaire, brochure and pricelist
Fifteen Factor Plus Questionnaire, Technical Manual
Fifteen Factor Plus Questionnaire, sample report
Fifteen Factor Plus Questionnaire, interview prompts report

OPQ 32

Background

The OPQ (Occupational Personality Questionnaire) was designed by, and is published by, SHL, the UK market leaders in occupational psychometric tests. There are a variety of versions of OPQ: the most popular are designed for senior and middle management, and these include the new OPQ 32r (reviewed here – the version reviewed for the first edition of this book was the Concept 4.2). Other popular models have been Concepts 3 and 5.2. These personality questionnaires analyse the typical behaviour of individuals in an occupational setting, and also have some input on the behaviour of individuals in groups. As with the 16PF and 15FQ+, the OPQ 32r test gives a useful, wide-ranging interpretation of an individual in the work setting. The original version of the OPQ had 30 scales, and then a revision introduced in 2000 was renamed OPQ 32, reflecting the addition of two more scales. This was sold in two versions: OPQ 32n – the 'normative' questionnaire – which asked people to rate themselves on a number of statements; and OPQ 32i – the 'ipsative' version that asked people to make forced choices between alternative statements.

The new OPQ 32r, launched in 2009, uses new developments in Item Response Theory to improve the way in which the questionnaire is scored, to be shorter and quicker to use, and to provide 'normative' scores from the forced-choice statement format. As SHL suggest, the style of the new OPQ 32r means that the test takes around half as long as it used to take, with the forced-choice item formats to control faking attempts and bias effects, and the normative scoring making interpretation quicker and easier. SHL claim that over the last ten years they have fully revised their range of tests more or less entirely.

SHL have worldwide rights to a number of useful personality questionnaires, mostly used in the past for selection purposes, but now also used for training and career development. OPQ is one of the most well-known of SHL's range of instruments. The range includes many other tests, used for a variety of purposes, including ability tests (see the discussion of Verify, above). SHL's tests are available in a number of languages: OPQ 32r has been adapted for use and normed in 31 languages.

The aims of the test

The OPQ is a personality test which aims to present a fuller picture of the individual than others on the market, while at the same time being user-friendly, and being clearly understandable by the non-Specialist. SHL would seem to have succeeded in this aim, and the OPQ tests are popular with many employers, executive search consultants and outplacement firms. OPQ 32, through its 32 different dimensions of personality, has proved itself to be especially useful in candidate selection. However, in practical terms it is more often used as a development tool than for recruitment.

This test is seen as highly job-relevant when incorporated with a job analysis to compare an individual with a job specification. The company has now designed 'competency-potential' reports, to convert the OPQ 32 scores into scores on the 20 competencies of their 'Universal Competency Framework'. The user in an organisation can now make a direct comparison between the competency requirements of a job and the predicted potential of a candidate who has completed the OPQ 32 – and can immediately spot the gaps and closeness of a match.

The format

In the OPQ 32r questionnaire, the testee is presented with blocks of statements in three parts, marked a), b), and c). Testees choose the statement which is most true or typical of their everyday behaviour, and then the opposite, or that which is least true. The administration and scoring of the test is completed online.

For example, take these three statements:

> *a)* *is assertive in groups,*
>
> *b)* *applies common sense,*
>
> *c)* *can sell ideas to a customer.*

The testee is asked to decide which statement is the most appropriate to him or her, and which is the least appropriate. Electronically, a scored result is produced almost immediately, including access to a wide range of reports based on the questionnaire and using different modes of analysis. These can be used to develop a clear profile of each candidate, for recruitment, development, etc.

Range of applications

Across a wide range of junior, middle and senior management functions – a very useful, widely-applicable exercise, especially with the possibility of matching to existing job competencies developed for specific jobs in a company. The reports provided with the OPQ32r are extremely insightful in analysing an individual's relationships with people, thinking styles and feelings and emotions, and there is also the possibility of matching the findings of the test against specific competencies (see below).

Doing the test

In doing the OPQ 32r, the person being tested is asked to think about each particular statement, and is then scored according to a certain norm group. While the earlier OPQ 32i was an ipsative test (see Glossary), the new scoring method with a mix of forced choice formats in the OPQr produces normative scales, which makes it quite unlike any other psychological tests on the market now.

As mentioned above, the test asks the testee to select "most like you" and "least like you" options – so choosing two of the three items in a block, and discarding the other.

The person being tested is asked to be as discerning and honest as possible, and not to give a certain response just because it seems the right thing to say (such as a socially desirable response), or how they might like the situation to be – as in the case of all tests reviewed in this book.

The test designers explain that they appreciate that, in some statement blocks, the statements may not be very relevant to a particular test-taker, and it may be difficult for him or her to choose the most appropriate option in order to answer the questions, but a decision must be made in each case. It is vital to complete all the questions and the testee should work fairly quickly without pondering at length any particular question.

Having said this, the test was quite challenging to take. It started with accessing the online version, with the need to remember to change the password. Then it is explained that the testee must choose two of the three from the 104 blocks of statements, either positively or negatively. It was occasionally necessary for the testee (during this review) to be reminded to complete each block due to forgetting the negative option, and there were times when it was difficult to choose a negative (all the options were "most like me" and it was difficult to choose the least of these). On the reverse side, there were occasions when all the options were "least like me", so the opposite problem arose. There did appear to be blocks of statements with too much similarity and not enough contrast, but this might have been a personal impression only. There also appeared to be extensive repetition of very similar statements or phrases.

Examples of content of the test

On each page on the screen there are two blocks of three statements. The task for the testee, as explained above, is to choose which statement is most like you and which is least like you in each block. When a block has not been completed, it is represented to the testee with the uncompleted choice clearly indicated.

I feel comfortable in formal situations   ○

I like to be active   ○

I generate creative ideas   ○

I enjoy the companionship of others   ○

I try out new activities   ○

I look to the future   ○

Time needed to complete the test

About 20-30 minutes, with around 70% of people completing the test in under 30 minutes.

Time to score the test

Immediately – the test is scored automatically and reports are then generated online. These can include both the OPQ profile and Manager Plus profile, linking the test results to the 20 universal competencies.

Necessary time for feedback

At least 30-45 minutes, ideally up to one hour per testee, by a trained test-user, who has completed the necessary administration and feedback skills training. This can be based on the very useful and clear reports provided.

Format/structure of the feedback

The profile chart relating to the OPQ 32r test analyses the personality profile of the testee, according to three main sectors: relationships with people, thinking style and feelings and emotions:

- Within **relationships,** the profile considers whether the testee is assertive, is gregarious and/or has empathy – the author came out as independent-minded, outgoing, socially-confident and caring;

- Under **thinking style,** the test looks at fields of use practiced by the testee, such as abstract thinking and structured thinking – the author's results saw her as behavioural in thinking, conceptual, detail-conscious and conscientious;

- Under **feelings and emotions** the profile examines reasons for anxieties, the practice of controls, and sources of energies – the author saw herself as relaxed, optimistic, emotionally-controlled, vigorous and decisive.

This produces a profile with 32 measures of personality, and also looks at the consistency of the responses as a check. The profile measures preferences according to a 'stens' scale, a psychologist's term for measuring preference strength. These profiles are presented along a stens scale of 1 to 10.

The OPQ also looks at **team types** and **leadership styles.** Under team types, the profile defines the extent to which the testee is one of the following eight types (based on the Belbin model): Coordinator, Shaper, Plant, Monitor/Evaluator, Resource Investigator, Completer, Teamworker and Implementer. Among the testee's **leadership styles**, the report looks at five types: directive leader, delegative leader, participative leader, consultative leader and negotiative leader. The profile also considers the individual's degree of adaptability. The OPQ also looks at **subordinate styles** under five headings: receptive subordinate, self-reliant subordinate, collaborative subordinate, informative subordinate and reciprocating subordinate.

The report, printed out as a result of the computer-scoring process and designed to be given to the person being tested, reiterates the profile chart and presents a short narrative analysing the main points of the profile in more detail. This is followed by a full report looking at the testee's relationships, thinking style, feelings and emotions. The SHL norm groups for the OPQ are large mixed groups, all of whom have tackled these questions over the last few decades. As we have seen, the OPQ is subject to constant revision and update, and there is now an international norm available that is based on over 370,000 people.

It is essential that people being tested should be normed against an appropriate peer group with profiles collected in SHL's research, otherwise their characteristics, which might appear average against their appropriate norm group, might be exaggerated against other norms. The standard SHL norm group is a large, professional graduate group.

As an experiment, a standard SHL norm was compared with a high managerial norm and a high-level female norm. How were they different? The same person being tested appeared to be much more persuasive in the basic norm than against the high-level norms. The same person was less controlling in the basic norm as well as more independent in the basic norm, less out going and less affiliative. Her level of social confidence was about the same in each. Modesty was lower in the high-level female norm and being democratic also scored lower in the high-level norms. Being practical scored higher in the high-level norms while being data rational was lower in the basic norms. Behavioural and conceptual thinking were much lower in the high-level female norm group but forward planning was higher in the basic norms. Critical feelings were higher in the basic norms, but competitiveness was lower in the high-level managerial norms while being achievement oriented and decisive were higher in the basic norms.

What does all this mean? The basic norms will indicate greater extremes, if the person is very much more achievement oriented, conscientious and persuasive, than in the large professional and graduate norm. In comparison with a high-level management norm, persuasiveness will be less extreme, and so will innovativeness and being achievement oriented. It is much more usual for a high-level management group to be more persuasive, more innovative, more critical and more achieving than a general management norm.

In the high-level female norm, where certain characteristics tend to be emphasised, there were other specific differences from the high-level management norm: the latter shows less independence, less modesty, more practical thinking, more of an artistic nature, more behavioural thought, less conceptual thinking, more forward planning, more worrying, less tough mindedness, less competitiveness and more achievement orientation.

Thus, the female norms show that this person is more competitive than the norm, more tough-minded, more innovative and more practical. However, she is less modest, and less behavioural in thinking, and less conceptual than typical high-level females.

These differences between norms are not particularly great, but they are significant, and again it should be stressed that it is important to be normed against your representative group as accurately as possible. It is unusual for the variants to be more than one or two stens (points on the scale) different, but where this occurs, such as where a person is very highly achievement oriented against basic norms, yet considerably lower against exact norms (in this case high-level female norms), the differences are obviously quite important.

The OPQ also offers the opportunity to classify a person according to their **selling styles** profile. This chart looks at the extent to which a person is product or people oriented in their sales approach, and the degree to which they are adaptable. Are they likely to perceive different requirements in different situations?

It is also possible to use the OPQ to analyse **behavioural styles,** which include:

confident communicator, a person who copes well in formal situations;

rapport creator, who quickly builds warm and friendly relationships;

culture fitter, who identifies and fits the prevailing customer culture;

culture breaker, a person valued for new ideas against the prevailing culture;

enthusiast, who infects customers with energetic enthusiasm;

perseverer, who succeeds by a determined persistence to achieve a sale;

business winner, who strives for success in a competitive situation;

technicians, who enjoy a technical style of selling;

administrative supporters, who reassure customers who feel a need to be assured of administrative quality and service;

and *team managers*, who understand how to assign, motivate and advise team members.

The OPQ **selling styles** also analyses how a person sells from the basis of interpersonal strengths and through building a relationship, their energy base, their level of energy and enthusiasm, and their thinking base and the degree to which they are rational. It is also possible to gain an idea of the extent to which the person is good in a general sales mode, and is able to sell in a variety of different ways. As mentioned above, the OPQ can also be linked to the use of the Belbin Team Types.

The OPQ is widely seen as a very powerful instrument, and if it is interpreted well it is far from superficial. The OPQ is capable of great insight and can be one of the most useful one-off tests, when there is no time to conduct a battery of tests on a candidate. A great many top psychologists use OPQ and, if used in a large validation study or linked to job analysis, it can be especially valuable. However, SHL's computer-generated summaries do not necessarily adequately replace individual, face-to-face feedback from a competent psychologist, and should not be used as a shortcut.

OPQ interpretation ideally should link the basic scales to give clearer insight into behaviour, and to produce team types or a user's own desired combinations of requirements. The quality of interpretation of SHL's OPQ when licensed out is inevitably not universally good, and poor interpretation has occasionally damaged the reputation of the instrument. SHL's reports can seem to be mechanistic and bland, especially in the case of a person who shows few extremes in their occupational personality.

The company has tried to add more value in its reports through producing not only the Premium Report, containing a summary of the implications of the findings, but a separate Team-Type and Leadership Report if required. For the OPQ 32r, the company can supply a Manager Plus Report; a Candidate Plus Report; a Universal Competency Report; a Sales Report; a Team Impact Report; a Management Competency Report; an Emotional Intelligence Report; a Development Action Planner and a Leadership Potential Report.

Value to the employer/user

As indicated, the OPQ can be an extremely useful general personality test for selection purposes, and can be used on its own (although with interviews and non-psychometric ways of assessment). It gains in value through more extensive use in a particular company. It is one of the most reliable and useful tests for a company with only a limited need for testing, and which does not necessarily want to develop an extensive battery of tests.

Value to the employee/person being tested

The OPQ test is among the most popular tests in widespread use, and having completed it once, the testee will be reasonably well prepared for other tests in the future. The OPQ helps people to become familiar with a wide range of testing concepts, including the Belbin Team Types. The OPQ helps in a preliminary understanding of working style and approach, and strengths and weaknesses in a corporate setting. In this respect, it is appropriate for people going through outplacement and preparing CVs, as it can build greater self-knowledge easily and quickly.

Value to the user organisation

The OPQ can help significantly in selecting people for appropriate corporate cultures, and in team-building. The results are in sufficient detail, in terms of work style and occupational characteristics, to predict the success or failure of certain individuals in certain organisations.

Those who are sufficiently self-reliant and individualistic to succeed in macho cultures are clearly apparent, as are those able to cope with the work pace of retail cultures. Personalities most suited for process cultures on the one hand, and high-risk, slow-feedback cultures on the other hand, will be visible in a quantifiable way, to a greater extent than in more basic personality tests, even in PAPI.

As mentioned, competency-based reports can also be generated from OPQ scores, describing the potential of a candidate in terms of the 20-dimension Universal Competency Framework, which can be directly related to job requirements in the organisation. In the author's competency report, she was identified as having strongest competencies in deciding and initiating action; creating and innovating; and coping with pressure and setbacks. She was seen as having only moderate strengths in leading and supervising, following instructions and procedures; and having entrepreneurial and commercial thinking preferences.

Can the test results be deliberately falsified?

With difficulty, because many of the statements do not appear to bear a close relation to the personality types being analysed, and a candidate trying to slant the answers in a certain way would find this difficult to sustain.

Also, in OPQ 32r, the testee has to choose 'most' and 'least' from three options which have apparently similar 'social desirability' or attractiveness. The need to focus on thinking through the testee's response to the test in a very deliberate way might make faking answers very challenging.

There is also the issue of the use of Verify – discussed before the test reviews – above.

Advantages over other tests

The OPQ has more detail and wider scope than the more basic tests. It can be used successfully on its own. Extensive norm groups have been developed, both for the UK and for many other countries, and for gender and management level. There is also extensive technical documentation available on the company's website, which can be freely downloaded. Few other psychological testing companies conduct such extensive research and validation. The reports are very detailed and presented in a user-friendly manner. The professionalism of the SHL approach comes out clearly in their documentation.

Disadvantages compared with other tests

The test can be seen to be superficial by a small minority of purist psychologists, but these are few and far between. OPQ also depends heavily on competent feedback, interpreting the reports. The use of computer-generated feedback has been criticised by some users, and obviously should not be depended on exclusively. Unless a user or testee is experienced in report interpretation, he or she should not rely exclusively on this when considering the results of the test.

Test may be combined with...

The OPQ can be used with more specific tests, such as the Thomas-Kilmann Mode of Conflict Inventory, and with conceptual thinking tests. It can be combined with SHL ability tests like the Verify range, and other tests from their stable, such as those examining career choices and motivation levels (see below).

Static/predictive value

The OPQ is widely seen as a good indicator of the outlook of a person, and is also useful in predicting behaviour in leadership or subordinate roles, or in teams. It is likely to be valid as a predictor for at least a year from the time of taking the test. The predictor of job-matching might also be superseded after one or two years. The comprehensive nature of this exercise increases its predictive value over several tests. The competency-link could be especially useful here.

Overall review

Speed of being tested – fast
Speed of scoring results – fast
Cost – low to medium
Range of applications – wide
In-house/Out-house – at SHL, or under license
Basic/Advanced – basic and advanced (the detailed reports can be used to generate advanced insights).

How to prepare yourself for sitting this test

Make sure that the instructions are fully understood, and that you are thinking in a working context, rather than socially or about your family. Be prepared to have to make decisions and choices which may not exactly express how you feel – so be flexible.

Will this test produce a different result after a period of time?

Possibly, and companies using the OPQ extensively will expect to be able to use an OPQ result for only about one year to 18 months.

Contact details: SHL, www.shl.com, UK@shlgroup.com, 0870 070 8000

Downloads: SHL White Paper 2009, The Occupational Personality Questionnaire Revolution: applying Item Response Theory to questionnaire design and scoring, by Anna Brown, Principal Research Statistician, and Professor Dave Bartram, Research Director

SHL OPQ32 Technical Manual, 2006

Motivation Questionnaire

Background

Many psychological testing providers have created instruments to measure motivation factors influencing employees. The SHL Motivation Questionnaire would seem to be one of the most popular and useful, produced by one of Britain's largest and most reputable testing providers, and in widespread use over the last decade. Extensive comparison group data is available. The reports provided – summarising individual inclinations and against norm groups – can be a useful tool for managers with teams.

The aims of the test

This test looks at important elements of motivation, suggesting which are likely to be the main motivators and de-motivators for a particular employee. As a self-reported questionnaire – like most of the tests featured in this book – the accuracy of the results depends on the frankness of the employee answering the questions, and his or her self-knowledge. Employers/bosses are recommended to focus on maximizing motivators and minimizing de-motivators, and are given advice according to each element identified. Although this test shows a high level of accuracy and reliability in usage, it is important for the employer or boss to confirm with the employee in a face-to-face discussion that these are indeed his or her motivators and de-motivators, and the impact on his or her current and future role at work.

The format

The test looks at a series of motivators and de-motivators, such as Achievement (wanting to overcome challenges and be obviously successful by hitting targets), Affiliation (making friendships at work and being part of a team), Autonomy (working alone and making individual decisions on approaches to work), Commercial Outlook (increasing sales, making profits and achieving obvious commercial success), Competition (the opportunity to be benchmarked and win against others), Ease and Security (work not too difficult and offering job security and pleasant working conditions), Interest (the work provides stimulation and is not boring), Level of Activity (being kept busy, with opportunities for multitasking and coping with pressure), Material Reward (offering attractive remuneration), Personal Growth (with opportunities to learn and acquire new skills), Personal Principles (not in conflict with personal ethics, quality standards, values and beliefs), Power (providing opportunities for responsibility and influence), Progression (offering prospects for promotion), and Recognition (with some kind of publicly-acknowledged reward or praise).

Possible de-motivators identified might include Fear of Failure (of not being able to achieve targets, of not being able to cope with criticism) and Immersion (or working beyond normal hours, of the job encroaching on personal time, of not having work-life balance, of having to travel in personal time). However, for some employees, Fear of Failure could spur them on to greater achievement. Some potential motivators and de-motivators, such as the need for Flexibility (the extent to which someone is motivated by the absence of clearly-defined structures and procedures for managing tasks) could be either/or, depending on the need for certainty or tolerance of ambiguity. Similarly, Status – the extent to which someone is motivated by outward signs of position and recognition of rank – may be motivational for some, but of no consequence to others.

In the test, questions are asked in all these areas, and the report accompanying the test analyses the positives and negatives of each motivation factor, with tips and suggestions for the employer or boss for improving motivation and decreasing de-motivation in each case.

Range of applications

This test could be useful in recruitment, especially for positions requiring a high level of self-motivation, and may also be valuable in an annual performance appraisal. Although a diligent manager might feel that he or she is perfectly aware of an employee's motivators and de-motivators, some of the results might still be surprising. The tips and suggestions in the computer-generated report would be especially useful when a manager is handing over to a successor and trying to make a briefing on staff members and the way to get the most out of them.

Doing the test

This test is usually administered online, but is also available in paper format. The testee is introduced to the test as a self-report questionnaire (as are most of the tests in this book) which is aiming to discover the sort of things which influence your motivation to work. There are 144 questions, with no time limits, but SHL suggest that 25 minutes should be sufficient.

The test is presented as a form of Likert scale, with five options for the testee to select from. A statement is presented and the testee is asked about the impact on his or her motivation:

It greatly reduces my motivation to work

It tends to reduce my motivation to work

It has no effect on my motivation to work

It tends to increase my motivation to work

It greatly increases my motivation to work

There are 24 screen pages to work through, with six statements in a block, with the Likert scale ranged next to each statement. The testee must click on one of five boxes next to the statement – a failure to complete a box is reminded by the computer programme, so it's not possible to progress until each page is finished.

The testee is warned that it may not be easy to complete all the scales as the testee's job may not be conventional. For example, it was difficult to complete in the case of this review, where the testee often worked from home or when on the road – not attending an office everyday – and when the testee works alone, rather than closely with colleagues. The exercise also seems to be geared to those working in a profit-making organisation. The blocks of statements do tend to appear to be rather repetitive after a while, as clearly the analysis of motivation is based on certain key motivation concepts, such as competitiveness, autonomy, fear of failure, ethical issues, praise, contribution, etc.

Examples of content of the test

As mentioned above, blocks of six statements are presented, with the testee forming an opinion according to the Likert scale for each, for example:

Being able to take my time over tasks	○ ○ ○ ○ ○ ○
Being unsure how my work relates to results in cash terms	○ ○ ○ ○ ○ ○
Being stimulated by the tasks in my job	○ ○ ○ ○ ○ ○
My work not challenging my abilities	○ ○ ○ ○ ○ ○
Being required to help other people	○ ○ ○ ○ ○ ○
Working in a fluid, unstructured environment	○ ○ ○ ○ ○ ○

Time needed to complete the test

Most people complete this test in under 30 minutes with around 20 minutes being average. Testees are encouraged not to dwell too long on each choice. The greatest problem (which takes time) might be the testee trying to relate the test to a particular job, especially one outside a normal setting.

Time to score the test

The test is scored automatically and the report is generated immediately, based on the respondent's choices in the questionnaire. This can then be the basis for the structured feedback session, as described below, for both the testee and his or her boss.

Necessary time for feedback

The respondent can read the report, but it should also be read by his/her boss, to gain ideas for managing this person more effectively. So for maximum value, the feedback should be for the person, their boss and their team. It would be all the more valuable if several employees were to take the test, and the feedback can be ongoing.

Format/structure of the feedback

The feedback to this test, included in the computer-generated report, includes useful tips and suggestions for employers and bosses managing an employee. These are divided into four categories: highly motivating, moderately motivating, highly de-motivating and moderately de-motivating. There is also a fifth category – areas of little or no impact on an employee.

For example, an employee identified as highly motivated by Autonomy, who wants to organise his or her own approach to work, needs to discuss with his or her boss what actually constitutes 'Autonomy' in practice. Then, the boss should take a "hands-off" approach, setting objectives and measures but letting the employee structure his or her own approach to the work. The boss should be sensitive to the employee's need for empowerment and not impose too many constraints. The employee needs support and resources to work independently, with agreed communication lines and frequency.

If the employee has a need for Power, he or she wants to exercise authority, take responsibility, negotiate deals, and be in a position to influence others. The boss and employee should discuss what this means in practice. The employee should be given opportunities to take on new responsibilities, get involved in decision-making, and express his or her opinions. This employee wants the chance to be in charge, and can be directed and helped towards encouraging and motivating others.

However, if the employee might be de-motivated by a Fear of Failure, and he or she is concerned about criticism and the loss of self-esteem, he or she would be happier working in a blame-free culture. His or her boss must not set objectives which are so unrealistic that the employee is unlikely to succeed, despite concerted effort.

The employee must be able to feel free to come to the manager with problems. The boss should be on the look-out for this employee feeling unconnected with a task. Balanced and constructive feedback must be offered, with sensitive handling of any shortcomings.

Value to the employer/user

This test would appear to offer considerable value to both testee and manager. The employee can know clearly in a carefully-defined way about his or her areas of motivation, which can help in volunteering for new projects and assignments – is this the kind of work I would like to do? The manager can sense with greater accuracy the mood and feeling of an employee when facing a task. In this review, the author saw herself as mostly motivated by opportunities for achievement, personal growth and autonomy.

Value to the employee/person being tested

This highly-focused test helps testees to decide not only what they see as their motivators, but what they may not care about one way or the other, and what may actually stop them from taking on new challenges. The former might be quite easy to identify, such as achievement, personal growth, recognition, etc. but the *de-motivators* may be less obvious. Are you concerned with not being able to achieve targets? Being criticised and finding it hard to cope with this? Are you worried about being so immersed in your work that you have no time for yourself? This test can help job candidates and employees to identify with what they are really looking for in a job.

Value to the user organisation

The organisation, armed with information on areas of motivation of employees, can plan task teams and delegations more successfully. Increased levels of motivation, and therefore of job satisfaction, productivity and general well-being could be achieved having tested people in the organisation, and managed them accordingly. At least major areas of de-motivation could be avoided. This would need sensitive and well-organised managers, but should be possible, at least to a certain extent. The motivation preferences could also be linked to the corporate culture, such as a desire for autonomy and achievement being linked to an entrepreneurial culture, for example. The user organisation can build up a profile of the motivation elements of its most successful staff, and look to attract this kind of person.

Can the test results be deliberately falsified?

There would be little point in a respondent doing this, as the test is designed to help him or her to achieve a happier and more productive work life. The discrepancy between test results and reality would soon be apparent to a sensitive manager.

Advantages over other tests

This test is focused particularly on motivation elements – these may be mentioned in other more general personality tests – but here there is an opportunity to analyse these factors in detail and come up with a result. So the main advantage of this test is its clear focus and target on this essential element of managing people in an organisation. The feedback for bosses as well as for respondents is another useful feature not necessarily common to other tests.

Disadvantages compared with other tests

Obviously, the results of this test reflect the choices of the respondent, which are highly subjective and depend on interpretation of the wording. They relate to the respondent's willingness to be frank and open, and to the extent of self-knowledge and self-awareness. But this would be the case in most psychometrics – the exception would be the use of scenario-based tests in an assessment centre.

Tests may be combined with…

This test could be part of a battery of tests with the OPQ or other tests from the SHL stable, or indeed any other general personality tests.

Static/predictive value

As a motivation questionnaire, the test has useful predictive value about how an employee would respond in a given situation –

would this task enhance motivation, or threaten to undermine it? It also helps explain how an employee feels about his or her job right now, as in a performance appraisal feedback session.

Overall review

Speed of being tested – fast
Speed of scoring results – fast
Cost – moderate
Range of applications – useful
In-house/Out-house – out-house, through a trained test administrator
Basic/Advanced – still fairly basic

How to prepare yourself for sitting this test

When taking the Motivation Questionnaire, the employee should think about his or her existing tasks – which are most enjoyable, exciting, make him or her feel good? If you are a candidate for a job, you should think generally about what you like doing or not. If the company to which you are applying is looking for someone motivated by quite different things, maybe this is not the organisation for you.

Will this test produce a different result after a period of time?

SHL suggest that the shelf-life of this test is around 18-24 months. If there are major changes in an employee's life or work he or she should be asked to complete the Motivation Questionnaire again.

Contact details: SHL, www.shl.com, UK@ shlgroup.com, tel. 0870 070 8000

Downloads: Motivation Questionnaire – Sample Report

FIRO-B or Fundamental Interpersonal Relations Orientation –B

Background

This questionnaire, originally developed just before the Second World War, was at first used for assessing US armed services recruits. Designed by Will Schutz PhD, FIRO-B dates back to 1958. The impetus for developing the theory and the questionnaires was obtained during Schutz's work at the US Naval Research Laboratory in 1952, in trying to understand the kind of people who can survive working and living together on board ships and submarines.

This 'standard' version has been recently updated and is available from OPP in a variety of languages (see contact details below). However, the version reviewed in the first edition of this book was copyrighted in 1987, and is known as 'Elements of Awareness-B', and was created by Schutz after he sold the rights to the original version. Both versions are considered and described here. The testee should enquire about which version he or she is taking.

The FIRO-B is a traditional psychometric tool covering a specific area of human psychology – interpersonal need. The range of FIRO questionnaires includes FIRO-B for behaviour (discussed below), FIRO-BC for children's behaviour, and FIRO-F for feeling. COPE (Coping Operations Preference Enquiry) looks at people's defence mechanisms in anxiety-provoking interpersonal situations. LIPHE (Life Interpersonal History Enquiry), looking at people's behaviour and feelings towards their parents, and VAL-ED (Education Values), are other FIRO products, the latter looking at the values a person holds about an educational situation. The most frequently-used version is based on the original FIRO-B, distributed by OPP.

FIRO-B examines a person's expressed behaviour but not what he or she actually wants to express. It examines what a person wants to get, but not what he or she actually gets. The 'Elements of Awareness-B' focuses on this latter dimension. Thus, the standard FIRO-B focuses on what the person wants, and the Elements add in what the person actually gets, acting as more of a diagnostic tool, reflecting Schutz's more experiential thinking at this point.

The aims of the test

The FIRO-B (strictly-speaking really a questionnaire more than a test) is designed to help people to become more aware of how they behave towards other people. The FIRO-B questionnaire revolves around three concepts:

- Being **included**, i.e. doing things with other people, and sharing;
- **Controlling**, i.e. taking charge and influencing;
- **Affection**, i.e. disclosing and telling true feelings ('Openness' in the Elements version).

Schutz's original idea was based around examining the difference between your reality as you perceive it, and what you would really like to be and to have. In the standard FIRO-B test, you are asked to identify what you see as your reality and what you would like to get from others. In the Elements version, you can then reappraise the questions according to what you would like to be true in your case (also possible in the standard FIRO-B feedback).

This questionnaire is therefore useful in analysing personal degrees of control, and tensions which may exist in people. It shows a difference between how things are perceived and how you would like them to be, especially in terms of your relationships with people, in the basic concepts of including, controlling and openness/affection.

The FIRO-B measures interpersonal need in a straightforward way (in contrast with the Elements version, less focused on measuring), analysing the levels of behaviour with which individuals feel comfortable, or 'correct', in relation to each person's needs for these three areas.

Schutz, in developing the FIRO-B, observed that much of the behaviour that is exhibited towards others is motivated by differing levels of needs for these three interpersonal dimensions, and research has substantiated their importance in human interaction.

The format

The standard FIRO-B looks at 54 statements, with nine for each of the six need areas. In the Elements version, the statements can be seen in both ways separately, i.e. as 'what I see' and 'what I want'. The 54 statements are listed in the centre of the self-scoring form, with 'what I see' on the left-hand side, and 'what I want' on the right. The standard FIRO-B, by contrast offers statements of varying intensity; testees rate the statements on a six-point scale. The FIRO-B is available online and in a pen and pencil version, which can be hand-scored in a self-scorable format.

As mentioned, the FIRO-B is designed to analyse the three dimensions of inclusion, control and openness. To what extent do you include others in your plans, and do you wish to be included in groups? To what extent do you exert control over others? To what extent do you control what you do and how you behave? How open are you with superiors, colleagues and subordinates?

The standard FIRO-B questionnaire gives a series of scores from 0-9 in each of the three interpersonal need areas, with a separate score for expressed and wanted needs, giving a total of six scores. It all adds up to create a person's profile, in terms of how they see themselves. Their satisfaction or dissatisfaction with their wanted goals and attributes is especially seen in the Elements version.

Range of applications

According to the FIRO-B accompanying literature, thousands of people have used the FIRO-B since 1958, including managers at all levels in virtually every type of business. FIRO-B is also used extensively in clinical psychology, with married couples, union workers, entrepreneurs, students, teachers, ministers of religion, military personnel, politicians, police officers, firemen, doctors, lawyers and many others, from all walks of life.

Doing the test

Testees must go through each statement systematically and consider to what extent this statement expresses reality for them, and indicate the choices made. This is the testee's perception of what they think is true. The testees undertaking the standard FIRO-B are asked about what they do and what they want to get.

The Elements version of the FIRO-B covers the other two dimensions, of what they want to do and what they actually get. The testee is then asked to reappraise each statement according to whether or not they would want this to be true. It is important to avoid the temptation to look at each statement in turn, decide if it is true and then if it is what you particularly want to be true.

Examples of content of the test

The statements presented in the standard FIRO-B ask if the testee likes to be with people; is honest with their close friends; is dominant when in company; is generally included in the activities of others; allows others to decide things for him or her; is able to influence other people's ideas; likes to join people doing things together; keeps part of himself or herself private. Many other statements of a similar nature are included to test the testee's sense of reality and what they want.

Examples of completing the test (reproduced here with permission from CPP) include:

Expressed behaviour: for each statement below, decide which of the following answers best applies to you. Place the number of the answer to the left of the statement. Please be as honest as you can.					
1. Never	2. Rarely	3. Occasionally	4. Sometimes	5. Often	6. Usually
Control	I try to be the dominant person when I am with people				
Inclusion	I try to include other people in my plans				
Affection	I try to have close relationships with people				

Wanted behaviour: for each of the next group of statements, choose one of the following answers.					
1. Nobody	2. 1 or 2 people	3. A few people	4. Some people	5. Many people	6. Most people
Control	I let other people control my actions				
Inclusion	I like other people to include me in their activities				
Affection	I like other people to act close and personal with me				

Time needed to complete the test

This test takes about 10-15 minutes and can be self-scored.

Time to score the test

Designed to be self-scored, and the results can be quickly analysed.

Necessary time for feedback

Can be around an hour, but can be shorter. At least 20-30 minutes would be necessary.

Format/structure of the feedback

The twelve scores of the Elements version relate to the six variables according to the actual profile and elements of satisfaction. They range from zero to nine, with the scores indicating the degree to which the person agrees with the statement, or endorses the need area most important to them. The standard FIRO-B looks at a scale of 1-6. The scores are a reflection of how the person has chosen to behave, up to now. The scores reflect a person's perception of their behaviour and take into account both frequency and selectivity of behaviour. For example, a low score might suggest that the person does not often show this behaviour, but also that he or she might be very selective about with whom they are comfortable showing this behaviour. It is emphasised in the FIRO-B scoring that the person has the ability to change, according to their desire and willingness to learn to change. The FIRO-B feedback suggests that if people find themselves responding angrily or defensively to one of the scores it could be that they believe, deep down, that this is an area of vulnerability for them.

The first part of the interpretation looks at the degree to which the person already **includes** other people in their life, and the degree to which they want to include people. They may be dissatisfied in terms of including more people than they want to, or wanting to include people more than they already do. The basis of FIRO-B Elements version is the indication of dissatisfaction, and a discrepancy between the perceived needs and what is already achieved. It can also be discussed in the standard FIRO-B feedback.

The second part of the profile analysis looks at how the person perceives **they are included** by other people in their activities. To what extent do people include me? Elements of dissatisfaction are shown (especially in the Elements version) in whether or not the person completing the test considers that people include them more than they want them to, or if the person wants them to include them more than they do already. The scores in each case in the Elements version show the extent of the discrepancy.

In the third element of the interpretation, the degree of **control** of other people is analysed. Do I control people, and do I want to control people, providing them with structure and direction? The degree of dissatisfaction is shown in terms of 'I control people more than I want to' and 'I want to control people more than I do'.

The fourth element of the profile looks at the extent to which the person feels that **they are controlled** by other people and how much they want people to control them (with structure and direction). They can be dissatisfied in so far as they are controlled by people more than they want them to, and if they want people to control them more than they do, especially in terms of a need for direction and structure.

The final two interpretation elements are about openness or affection. To what extent am **I open** with people? To what extent do I want to be open with people? On the negative side, a person can be more open with people than they want to be, or can want to be more open with people than they are already. In the last interpretative element, the person responding to the instrument considers whether or not **people are open with me**, and if I want people to be open with me. On the dissatisfaction scale it can be concluded whether or not the person feels that 'People are open with me more than I want them to be' or 'I want people to be open with me more than they are'. The standard FIRO-B talks about 'Affection' rather than 'Openness'.

So, the basis of the standard FIRO-B is the division of each interpersonal dimension into:

a) what behaviour is seen to be most comfortable, and is most commonly exhibited towards other people; and

b) what behaviour is felt to be required in relationships with other people.

The FIRO-B test divides each interpersonal dimension into two aspects:

1. **expressed behaviour,** or how individuals believe they behave toward others; and

2. **wanted behaviour,** or how individuals want others to behave towards them (which is often harder to see in an obvious way).

Therefore, each individual will show either expressed or wanted behaviour for inclusion, control and affection. The expressed aspect of each dimension relates to aspects of behaviour seen as most comfortable in using towards others to bring people together (referred to as 'expressed inclusion'), in order to get our own way in what we want ('expressed control') and what we do to be close to others ('expressed affection').

On the other hand, the wanted element of each dimension of behaviour refers to how we want others to treat us in their attitude towards relationships with us ('wanted inclusion'), to get their way ('wanted control') and to be close in their relationship to us ('wanted affection').

'**Expressed inclusion**' means that we want to include other people in our way of life at work or socially and be included in theirs. This also means we want to belong to social or work groups and have the company of other people as much as possible.

'**Expressed control**' refers to trying to exert control and influence over things, to taking charge of things and telling other people what to do.

'**Expressed affection**' means that we try to become close to people, that we express friendliness and try to show personal warmth in relationships.

'**Wanted inclusion**' means that we tend to want other people to include us in their activities and to invite us to belong, even if we do not make much of an effort to be included.

'**Wanted control**' refers to us needing others to control us and wanting others to influence us, and sometimes even tell us what to do.

'**Wanted affection**' defines feeling of wanting others to express friendliness and personal warmth towards us, and wanting others to be close to us.

According to Ed Musselwhite, in a pamphlet describing the interpretation of FIRO-B results, published by the Consulting Psychologist Press of California, this test helps in understanding individual levels of needs with respect to the interpersonal dimensions. We have a sense that 'all is right in our interpersonal world' when our needs are met in our relationships at about the levels that we view as 'correct' and comfortable for ourselves, based on our unique life experiences.

If we experience more than our preferred comfortable level of one or more of these dimensions, we may feel we are being crowded, pushed, or smothered. If we experience less than our preferred, comfortable level of one or more of these dimensions, we may have feelings of being left out, of being without proper direction, or of being rejected, unloved or unappreciated.

Individual FIRO-B scores can vary dramatically on the dimensions; some people being tested will have almost all low scores; some will have mixed high, low and middle range scores; and some have scores near the middle of the range for almost all dimensions.

The need for each 'interpersonal dimension' can be seen as an important personal preference within a relationship. There is a tendency to fall into a blaming, attacking or retreating role with others when a preferred level of need is not being met. This can be coped with if it is possible to understand why a person is behaving in this way.

Unless we have some understanding of what we want from others in regard to the three dimensions, it is all too easy to miss important opportunities to build and maintain relationships that could be satisfying for everyone concerned. When things are going well, we may be pleased, but unclear about how we got there; when things are going badly, we may not have a meaningful awareness of what has changed or how to go about creating the good times again.

A closer view of inclusion, control and affection, and their expressed and wanted aspects is explained in the feedback session, as each person's FIRO-B scores, revealed in the Guttman scale – which has been validated and tested – indicate 'how much' each interpersonal dimension seems comfortable for each person. In the feedback session, the person doing the test can be asked additional questions, according to 'how much' they consider each of a series of questions to be relevant.

Some of these other questions overlap, and other questions could be added to them. But the person administering the test may use these as additional contexts to help you understand your FIRO-B scores. FIRO-B looks at expressed behaviour but not at what is wanted to be expressed, and at what people want to get but not at what they do get.

Thus, FIRO-B looks at inclusion from the point of view of 'I include people', control from 'I control people' and affection from 'I am open with people'. Then it looks at aspects of wanted behaviour in terms of 'I want people to include me', 'I want people to control me', and 'I want people to be open with me'. It also looks at wanted behaviour in terms of 'I want to include people', 'I want to control people', and 'I want to be open with people'. It also looks at what a person actually gets: 'People include me'; 'People control me'; 'People are open with me'.

As an alternative to the standard FIRO-B (itself substantially updated), the FIRO-B Elements of Awareness-B has been revised to add to the basic questionnaire, especially in terms of two further aspects for consideration, called 'perceived' and 'received'. It complicates and lengthens the questionnaire but adds important new elements.

Value to the employer/user

An employer needs to know how you can work with others, both more senior and more junior, and how you can find a way of interacting so that you can accommodate everyone's different preferences. FIRO-B is useful in team-building and especially in career development exercises, and in developing sound relationships. It is also used as a selection tool. Understanding actual, perceived and preferred behaviours can affect relationships profoundly, and these findings can be applied with some value in a working environment.

Behaviour preferences can have significant impact on the success of interpersonal relationships. The degree to which an interpersonal relationship is mutually successful tends to reflect, to a certain extent, the degree to which that relationship provides the amount of inclusion, control and affection that each person prefers. The FIRO-B helps to define these, and discrepancies can be rectified, especially through increased self-awareness and thus greater freedom of interpersonal awareness.

Value to the employee/person being tested

FIRO-B can help many of those using it to improve their understanding of how to improve their relationships with others. Clearly, this is vitally important to almost everyone and FIRO-B claims to have proven success in helping this understanding. It certainly complements other tests well, and adds quite a different dimension. This test looks as how aware a person is in terms of the way they deal with other people. It looks at wanted behaviour compared with actual behaviour, and looks quite deeply into a field of perception which other tests do not necessarily consider. It may show considerable differences between how you behave and how you want to behave.

The FIRO-B test can reveal to someone who comes out low on affiliation and caring that they are actually more or less sensitive, tolerant and considerate than he or she thought they were. In this sense, it is very usefully combined with more occupationally driven tests, which may fail to emphasise this aspect.

Value to the user organisation

FIRO-B can help people to fit into specific organisations, in terms of its input on relationships. Controlling types will fit well into macho cultures, whereas including types will prefer process cultures. Open types will work well in high-risk, slow-feedback cultures. Retail (work hard/play hard) cultures tend to attract including types, and those who want to be controlled.

Can the test results be deliberately falsified?

Possibly, but the person doing the test is asked not to see the scores as judgements, but just as ways of becoming more familiar with themselves. As this test is about relationships, it would be pointless to pretend to be a different type, because this would soon become obviously inaccurate. Many people doing this test might find it confrontational and may be in denial of the results during the feedback session.

Advantages over other tests

Gives insights into relationships, and can examine feelings and sensitivities more clearly than many other tests. Even though the original standard version of this test is now quite old (although substantially revised) it is still regarded as a classic – see the Leadership Report with the standard FIRO-B linked to the MBTI in Downloads (below).

Disadvantages compared with other tests

FIRO-B has been regarded as rather American in style and rather trite in terms of the provided interpretive comments. It would need to be combined with other tests to produce a wider view, especially in the occupational context. However, updated European versions are being developed, including in UK English.

Of course, it does look at a limited range of characteristics of the testees, so this might be seen as another disadvantage.

Tests may be combined with...

The FIRO-B can be combined with the OPQ, Myers Briggs Type Indicator, 16PF and more specific tests such as the Thomas-Kilmann.

Static/predictive value

Looks at the perceptions of the individual at a given point in time, and it may not be so useful predicatively because these could change. However, it could be useful in predicting attitudes to the specific elements of inclusion, control and openness.

Overall review

Speed of being tested – fast
Speed of scoring results – fast
Cost – low
Range of applications – narrow due to focus on specific behaviours
In-house/Out-house – in-house, under license
Basic/Advanced – basic

How to prepare yourself for sitting this test

No particular preparation is needed, but testees can think about their relationships at work rather than just with people they meet socially, considering their attitudes to including, controlling and being open.

Will this test produce a different result after a period of time?

After a period of time the test might be different, if the person subsequently feels more or less isolated, or is put into a different working environment.

Contact details: OPP, www.opp.eu.com, tel. 0845 603 9958 for the standard FIRO-B.

Downloads: Eugene R. Schnell, Leadership Report using the FIRO-B and MBTI Instruments, Report Presented for Test Case 107102009, Oct 07, 2009 – www.cpp.com

FIRO-B Profile Report – sample (based on the standard FIRO-B)

TKI or Thomas-Kilmann Mode of Conflict Instrument

Background

This questionnaire, devised in the USA but used in the UK for selection and career development exercises, dates back to the mid-1970s and stems from Kenneth Thomas's study, *Conflict and Conflict Management* (see Further Reading), which was published within a general study of industrial and occupational psychology. This instrument may be best suited for the American market for which it was designed, but nevertheless it is highly relevant in any other Western/industrialised corporate context. The instrument is the result of a collaboration of Kenneth Thomas and Ralph Kilmann, the latter still an active researcher and contributor to the field, who has most recently worked on developing diagnostic tools to manage conflict.

Few general tests cover this important area of conflict in such detail and in such a useful and practical way. It has important applications beyond studying the conflict preferences of individuals in organisations, to analysing behaviours of negotiators and politicians, for example.

The aims of the test

The Thomas-Kilmann Conflict Mode Instrument looks at how a person would respond in debate and discussion, particularly in an area of disagreement. What happens when a person's wishes differ from those of the majority? What are the different strategies for dealing with conflict available? What is the most popular or commonly-used preference of a person facing a conflict situation?

The person being tested is asked to consider how to respond to a conflict situation in which they find themselves, their wishes and attitudes different from those of another person or group of people. The instrument basically helps us to diagnose how to deal with people, in terms of how relationships and information are used in handling a conflict.

The Thomas-Kilmann exercise shows how people behave in conflict. How politically sensitive are they? Do they treat people with diplomacy or do they lack tact? Do they use bargaining and trading to get things done? Do they keep sight of the larger issues in spite of the outbreak of conflict? How much are they prepared to give in? Do they sometimes appear unreasonable?

The format

The testee is asked to respond to a specific set of 30 pairs of statements listed on a sheet with a) or b) options, and is asked to circle a) or b) on the answer sheet according to how they would expect to behave in a conflict situation. A calculation of the choices reveals the most popular preferences for each testee.

Of the five possible ways of approaching a situation of disagreement, usually two or three are popular with each respondent, with one or two being low preferences, and possibly one or two moderate preferences. The five ways of approaching conflict (discussed in detail below) are competitiveness, collaboration or cooperativeness, accommodating, avoiding and compromising.

Range of applications

This instrument can be used for general management selection and career development purposes. It is also useful for selection of senior candidates for leadership roles. It may also have other applications in understanding negotiating and bargaining styles, useful in sales situations, for example.

Doing the test

The test statements are uncomplicated, and it is usually a simple issue to decide which are the most appropriate – A or B. The statements do not necessarily relate to conflict situations, but do reveal attitudes. As a result, the face validity is fairly high.

Examples of content of the test

Testees are asked to choose between A and B options. They decide which of the two applies most to them. Examples (reproduced here with permission from CPP) include:

A. *I am usually firm in pursuing my goals*

B. *I attempt to get all concerns and issues immediately out in the open*

A. *I might try to soothe other's feelings and preserve our relationship*

B. *I try to do what is necessary to avoid tensions*

A. *I propose a middle ground*

B. *I am nearly always concerned with satisfying all our wishes*

Time needed to complete the test

About 10-15 minutes, up to 20 minutes.

Time to score the test

This test, taken as a pen-and-paper exercise, can be quickly scored manually on a prepared sheet by the person administering the test, involving adding up scores for each of the five conflict modes and identifying the areas of high and low preference. The instrument is also available online with computer-generated scoring, which also produces a report. This is a very quick and easy exercise, useful in training as well as in selection and development.

Necessary time for feedback

About 20-30 minutes is usually sufficient to discuss the attitude of the testee to conflict, especially if the testee thinks this is a fair assessment.

Format/structure of the feedback

The test, which comprises 30 questions, looks at five areas of handling conflict: competing (forcing); collaborating (problem-solving); compromising (sharing); avoiding (withdrawal); and accommodating (smoothing). How does the person taking the test rate themselves according to each method or approach of dealing with conflict?

In scoring, the test-taker or testee is given marks for each of these attitudes toward conflict. Therefore, the 30 questions actually break down into six groups of questions, tackling each different attitude, randomly mixed up in the test.

The scores show, for example, how competitive a person may be in forcing the discussion towards their desired outcome in a conflict situation. The preferences reflected in the scores show the following:

1. *How collaborative a person is in working with others to achieve a solution to the problem in hand, rather than trying to score points off the other people in the team*

2. *How much the person is prepared to compromise to get a solution*

3. *The extent to which the person is able to share ideas and strategies with others, in the interests of accomplishing the tasks*

4. *Whether or not the person tends to implement avoiding tactics, and withdraw from potential conflict, when possible. Would the person rather get as far as possible from the dispute and remain outside, even though this means that the opportunity to help make the decision is lost?*

5. *How accommodating a person is in terms of using the ideas of other people and taking note of their wishes to avoid conflict. Is there a tendency to try to minimise disputes by calming everyone down? Is the respondent happy for everyone to get their say?*

Various academic studies have shown that the five conflict-handling modes are apparent in all conflict situations, defined as incidents when the concerns of at least two people working together appear to be incompatible. In these situations it is possible to describe a person's behaviour in two basic dimensions: first, assertiveness, i.e. the extent to which the individual attempts to satisfy his own concerns and, secondly, cooperativeness, i.e. the extent to which the individual attempts to satisfy the other person's concerns. The five conflict-handling modes can be seen within these two dimensions, and can be plotted in a matrix to this effect.

For example, a person who is very competitive is at the top of the assertiveness scale and at the bottom of the cooperativeness scale. A person who is accommodating is at the bottom of the assertiveness scale but at the top of the cooperativeness scale. A collaborating person is at the top of the cooperativeness scale, but is also at the top of the assertiveness scale. Someone who is avoiding any kind of conflict at all is both unassertive and uncooperative. Compromising is exactly in the middle of all the scales. It is unlikely that a person can be both competing and collaborative, or avoiding and accommodating, i.e. they will be either assertive or unassertive. People who are either assertive or unassertive could also be compromising. It is likely that a high score in assertive qualities will be matched by low scores in avoiding and accommodating, and vice versa. Being highly competitive and highly accommodating at the same time is fairly unusual.

It is also possible to see the five conflict preferences in win/lose dimensions. Competing is win/lose – someone wins, and someone else must lose. Accommodating, the opposite, is lose/win. The person has deliberately chosen to let the other person win, which is in contrast with avoiding – this is when the person has chosen to walk away from the conflict, and is taking a lose/lose approach. Compromising can be seen as a combination – win/lose, lose/win and lose/win, win/lose. Both parties are winning and losing, depending on the particular points they are succeeding in gaining or giving away.

How are each of the five types defined? According to the literature provided with the instrument:

- A **competitive** person is in a power-oriented mode using whatever power seems appropriate to win, including ability to argue, pull rank on another, and exert economic sanctions. Competing can mean standing up for your beliefs or just trying to win, but it is done at the other person's expense.

- **Accommodating** means a person neglecting his or her own concerns to satisfy the concerns of the other person or people. Accommodating involves self-sacrifice, selfless generosity or charity, and yielding to another's point of view even if it clashes with your own.

- **Avoiding** involves the individual not pursuing their own concerns or those of anyone else, and refusing to address the conflict at all. Avoiding may mean diplomatically sidestepping an issue, postponing an issue until another time or simply withdrawing from a threatening situation altogether.

- **Collaborating** involves an attempt to work with the other person to find a solution which satisfies both of them. It involves probing an issue to identify the underlying interests of the people in conflict. Collaborating may take the form of exploring a disagreement from each other's point of view, concluding to resolve some condition which would otherwise have them competing for resources, or confronting the difficulties and trying to find a creative solution to an interpersonal problem.

- **Compromising** means finding some expedient and mutually acceptable solution which at least partially satisfies both parties. Compromising gives up more than the competing mode, but less than when accommodating. It addresses an issue more directly than avoiding, but does not explore it in the same depth as in the collaborating mode. Compromising may mean dividing differences, exchanging concessions or seeking a middle ground position.

All five conflict modes can be useful in certain situations. The effectiveness of a given conflict-handling mode depends upon the specific situation and the way in which the mode is used. Everyone has an ability to use all five modes, although some predominate because of temperament or practice. How useful is each mode? Again, the literature explaining the use of the conflict modes suggests that:

The **competing mode** is useful in emergencies and also where unpopular things must be done, like cost-cutting and implementing disciplinary measures. A competing mode can help you to protect yourself against someone trying to take advantage of you. If you scored high in a competing mode, one problem might be that you are surrounded by yes-men, people who agree with you because they have learned that it is unwise to disagree with you. This can stop you from receiving vital information. Are subordinates afraid to admit ignorance and uncertainties to you? Are people therefore less able to learn from you?

If you **scored low in competition,** it could mean that you often feel powerless in situations. It may be that you are unaware of your power or are unable to use it. Do you have trouble taking a firm stand? This may be because you're concerned with others' feelings or the use of power gives you problems.

The use of the **collaborating mode** is an important way to find a solution when you cannot easily compromise between your concerns and those of others. Collaborating helps you to learn by testing your own assumptions and understanding the inputs of others, helping in the merging of insights from people with different perspectives. Collaborating can help gain commitment through consensus, and can help to get over problems in interpersonal relationships. However, those people who score high on collaborating should ask themselves if they spend too much time discussing issues in depth, which perhaps do not deserve such time expenditure. Collaboration takes a good deal of time and energy, and consensus decision-making can sometimes represent a desire to minimise risk, by diffusing responsibility and delaying action. You should also ask yourself whether or not your collaborative behaviour succeeds or fails to encourage collaborative responses from others. In a conflict situation others may disregard collaborative overtures, and the trust and openness which you exhibit in being collaborative may be abused. You may be seen as too friendly and soft, and may miss indications of defensiveness, impatience, competitiveness and conflicting interests.

If you scored **low on collaborating,** you may not be able to see differences as opportunities to help solve problems. If you don't like conflict at all, this mindset can prevent you from seeing collaborative possibilities, and can stop you from having the satisfaction of helping in a successful collaboration. A person low on collaboration may find that subordinates are not committed to their decisions, as perhaps their concerns are not being included.

The **compromising mode** is useful when goals are moderately important to each person but not worth risking the potential breakdown of a relationship when using the more assertive modes, such as competitiveness. Compromising is also useful when two opponents with equal power are strongly keen on goals in conflict with each other. Compromising can achieve temporary settlements to complex issues, and can help the parties to arrive at expedient solutions under time pressure. Compromising can be a useful back-up mode when attempts at collaborating or competing are not working. But if you scored high in compromising you should ask yourself that by focusing on the practicalities of compromise, perhaps you are losing sight of the larger issues, such as core values and long-term objectives. Does an emphasis on bargaining and trading concessions create a cynical climate? Such a result might undermine interpersonal trust and deflect attention away from the merits of the issues.

If you scored **low on compromising** you may find yourself too sensitive or embarrassed to be effective at bargaining. You may also find it hard to make concessions and then have trouble avoiding mutually destructive arguments and power struggles.

The **avoiding mode** is useful in the case of unimportant issues, especially when more important issues are pressing and you have no chance of influencing the situation. When the potential damage of confronting a conflict is greater than the benefits of resolving it, avoiding can be a useful mode. The avoiding mode is also good for reducing tensions when people need to cool down. It is also appropriate when it is necessary to gather more information before coming to a decision. The avoiding mode could be used when others can resolve the conflict more effectively and when the issue might be outside of your responsibility. If you scored high on avoiding it may be that others will have problems gaining your input. Are you using too much energy avoiding issues rather than facing and resolving them? Are decisions on important issues made by default?

If you scored **low on avoiding** you may find yourself hurting people's feelings or stirring up problems where they did not exist.

You may need to be more discreet and tactful to avoid causing more conflict. If you are too busy in your workplace, overwhelmed by too many issues, it may be that you should avoid more. You may need to plan more to set priorities, and delegate more important issues.

Accommodating is useful when you realise that you are wrong. This allows you to show that you can be reasonable. Accommodating is appropriate when the issue being discussed is more important to the other person. It then appears as a goodwill gesture, helping to maintain cooperative relationships, building friendships for future benefit. The accommodating mode is best when continued competition would damage your cause, or when it is most unlikely that you can win. Accommodating helps to preserve a harmonious environment, and helps subordinates to try things by themselves and learn from their own mistakes. However, if you are high on accommodating you may feel that your own ideas are not getting much attention. Allowing others to keep advancing their concerns can deprive you of influence, respect and recognition. Your own contribution will not be obvious. Those who score high on this attribute may not be able to effectively impose discipline at work.

If you scored **low on accommodating**, you may have trouble building up goodwill with other people, who may see you as unreasonable. Can you admit when you are wrong? You should ask yourself if you recognise legitimate exceptions to rules, and when to give up your line of argument.

Value to the employer/user

This instrument is a good discussion tool in analysing how the testee deals with people in a potential conflict situation. Are they good at collaborating? Or do they see everyone as being a competitor? Do they compromise, avoid or accommodate? In a leadership role, it is essential for the attitude towards conflict to be clearly understood, within the context of the team for which a person is to be hired, or in which he or she works already. There are interesting cultural variations when this exercise is being used in different companies, or in different countries. Strong tendencies towards compromise and avoiding in a particular group are indicative of a culture where people do not feel it possible to stand up for what they believe, and where problem-solving is not seen as a rewarded behaviour.

Value to the employee/person being tested

The Thomas-Kilmann instrument provides a new way of looking at how conflict is dealt with, and the feedback is invaluable in explaining the positives and negatives of each conflict mode to the respondent, and the impact on his or her job and way of operating. The testee can be in a better position to analyse when the use of a certain conflict mode is most appropriate, based on the nature of the conflict itself. Everyone has an element of each mode within their characteristics – even if it is comparatively subdued – and can use this to the maximum when required. The test helps people to realise that their usual conflict mode is not always suitable, and to learn to be more adaptable. The cores of a person tend to reflect the corporate culture of their organisation and national context, as much as personality.

Value to the user organisation

As we have seen above, this instrument is especially valuable in providing a working definition to these attitudes to conflict, which can be very useful in matching a person to a specific corporate culture. Some cultures prefer very competitive people, while others seek those who are more accommodating. The macho culture company would look for people who are in competing mode and, to a certain extent, people who are compromising, in terms of the fact that in macho cultures, there is a need for results-oriented people who are dedicated to completing the task in hand. A process culture would prefer people who are accommodating and avoiding. A retail culture would seek competitive people, and a high-risk, low-feedback culture would look for collaborating preferences, combined with accommodating skills. A job needing problem-solving would benefit from a person with collaborative preferences, with this person welcoming problems as opportunities to learn, rather than as annoying disruptions that should be "fixed" as soon and as easily as possible.

Can the test results be deliberately falsified?

This test could only be falsified with difficulty, because of the variety of the statements and the random way in which the different modes are tested. It would also be very inappropriate to try to come over as having an unnatural conflict mode, because this could not be sustained in situations of real conflict. In the feedback session, testees can often be asked for examples of behaviours to confirm their choices.

Advantages over other tests

The exercise contains more detail on how conflict is handled than most other tests, and provides a clear way of defining the main attitudes to conflict. Those familiar with the test can use it to see what is happening in a conflict situation. The simplicity of this test and ease of gaining familiarity with the concepts can add value in identifying workplace behaviours and attitudes, more so than other more complex instruments.

Disadvantages compared with other tests

This test looks only at conflict modes and does not consider other aspects of personality, so it needs to be accompanied by other tests to reveal further dimensions. Rather American in style, it may face some user-resistance in the UK.

Tests may be combined with...

The Thomas-Kilmann exercise may be combined with the MBTI, OPQ, 16PF or 15FQ+, in order to gain a more complete picture of a person.

Static/predictive value

Good indicator of how a person will behave in a conflict situation, as well as indicating subsidiary conflict modes which can be drawn on when needed.

Overall review

Speed of being tested – fast
Speed of scoring results – fast
Cost – low
Range of applications – wide
In-house/Out-house – in-house, can be licensed-in
Basic/Advanced – basic

How to prepare yourself for sitting this test

It can be useful to think of the conflict situations in which you have recently been involved. How did you react? Do you nearly always react in a certain way, or are you quite adaptable? Do you welcome conflict as a normal part of the working day, or see it as a fairly rare occurrence which you would not greet with much enthusiasm? Do you enjoy a fight, or run away from what looks like a potentially nasty situation? Your attitudes will come through in this exercise, and they can be used positively or negatively in the workplace.

Will this test produce a different result after a period of time?

Possibly, but unlikely to be very different, unless the person has experienced a completely contrasting work environment from before, in which conflict is either much more common or much less apparent. Visiting another country and working there for a length of time might also lead to different preferences. It can be that a person liked to be collaborative, but found this to be difficult in a new environment, and so used the compromising mode more frequently.

Contact details: OPP, www.opp.eu.com, tel. 0845 603 9958

Downloads: Robert McHenry: Fight, Flight or Face It? Celebrating the effective management of conflict at work, a CIPD Report, July 2008
Product fact sheet: The Thomas-Kilmann Mode of Conflict Instrument
Thomas-Kilmann Mode of Conflict Instrument – profile and interpretative report

Raven's Progressive Matrices

Background

This is an abstract reasoning test, traditional, well-established, and with extensive norm groups, which aims to test general mental ability. Norms for Raven's Matrices have now been developed in many countries of the world, and some for specific age, ethnic and occupational groups. It can be used as a learning ability, job performance and intelligence test, but it is included here because of its increasingly common use in the testing of strategic thinking and problem-solving ability. As a non-verbal test, it can be used for assessing people from a wide range of cultural backgrounds, and shows no linguistic bias.

When John Raven (a psychologist based in Edinburgh) devised the tests in the 1930s, he was convinced that better results were obtained when it was untimed, but there has been wide demand for their use in group setting where convenience dictates that everyone should finish the test together. When the test is timed, it should be normed against timed norms. The tests have been developed over more than 30 years, with the initial series first published in 1938 and the second series in 1947. Each series has been revised in the light of more research.

Raven's Progressive Matrices have been devised to be used with other tests, especially with tests of verbal and numerical reasoning, such as the Watson Glaser (see below).

The aims of the test

Raven's Progressive Matrices are very well-known ability tests, which can also be used to reveal a great deal about thinking conceptually and autonomously. They question strategic thinking capacity, and the ability to stand back and look at a problem from a distance. In many cases, psychologists use Raven's as an intelligence test, but others use it as an approach to problem-solving, especially when the person is asked to explain why they made a certain choice. Senior executive selection processes often include Raven's when there is a need for a visionary approach in a position being headhunted. Raven's is used frequently in the recruitment of scientists and IT professionals.

The test is called 'progressive' because it becomes progressively harder as the testee moves through the exercise.

The format

Raven's Progressive Matrices – the version reviewed for this book – consists of 36 puzzles. Each puzzle has three rows of three designs, with a final one missing. It is necessary to use increasing intellectual judgement to decide on the continuing image to fill in the gap. This must be based on what has gone before, and a series of options are given below the design to be completed, from which the testee must choose. The puzzles are all visual images, based on different shapes and forms, both complete and incomplete, in outline form and solid. People with strong conceptual ability will immediately feel at home with these. They are available with the instructions in a range of languages.

Two new abbreviated versions are available online – the Advanced Progressive Matrices for senior level managers and advanced individual contributors, and the Standard Progressive Matrices for supervisor-level staff.

Range of applications

The test is mainly used to gauge mental ability, as an intelligence test for general use, or specifically in senior executive selection to test strategic and conceptual thinking patterns. Raven's can be easy to use and can give easily comparable results. It can also be used at more junior levels.

Doing the test

This test requires a good sense of logic and strategic thinking in order to gain a high score. Many accountants, engineers and also senior executives in strategic planning roles enjoy doing these tests and gain high scores.

Raven's Progressive Matrices can be used at the outset of an assessment to analyse the basic intelligence of the person being tested. Within the first few minutes it is clear whether or not the person being tested comes within the 'dullest' 10 per cent of adults, the 'average' 80 per cent, or the 'brightest' 10 per cent. This is ascertained from doing the first problem of the set, which takes only a few moments. If a person makes a mistake at any stage of the initial test they are warned that they should look closely at the pattern to remember that one – and only one – of the pieces shown is right, and to be sure that a choice is made of the one which makes the pattern correct both along and down the scales. This exercise with an initial, practice test is useful in giving the person doing the test some confidence that they know what they are doing.

In doing this test, the approach of the testee to the problems within the series of 36 puzzles is seen as particularly revealing, and the tester or person administering the test will question the testee as to the logic behind the choices made. They may be asked to reason through their selection of the answer to this specific problem and this reveals not only the logic they used to answer the problem, but in some degree the confidence they have in their own judgement.

Some people, especially those who are very competitive, will argue against the tester even when they are told they are wrong. The way in which the problem is approached often shows that someone may be on the right track at the beginning of the test or situation but fails to follow through.

Doing abstract problems means that each problem must be solved separately, and after it has been completed, you must move on from the thinking behind that solution. You must look at each problem freshly, as it will require a different way of thinking. Pattern recognition is always required.

When working at speed some people attempt a large number of problems, and guess at the answers when they do not clearly see the solution. Others prefer to tackle fewer problems, but make fewer mistakes, making certain that they have solved each problem correctly before going on to the next. In either case, the output of efficient intellectual activity appears to be almost the same, according to studies of Raven's results over the years.

The main difference is that the former approach uses up more of the test material in the allotted 40 minutes, and cannot greatly increase the score when the person taking the test is allowed to go on working until they have finished. The maximum output of efficient intellectual work involves using both material and time well.

Example of content of the test

(Not possible for copyright reasons, but see description above for a 'feel' of the exercise.) One example is given in the fact sheet (see Downloads). There are eight shapes in rows of three, with the ninth left blank. The testee has to choose the uniquely-correct shape to fill the blank space from a choice of eight shapes. The correct shape fills the gap both vertically and horizontally.

Time needed to complete the test

Forty minutes, strictly timed, on the occasion when the exercise was reviewed. This could be longer or shorter, depending on the norms used. According to general recommended practice, the Advanced version, with 23 items, should take 42 minutes, including two minutes for practice; the Standard version, with 28 items, should take 47 minutes. This should be strictly timed. A range of normative data is available at these timings.

Time to score the test

Scoring can be completed rapidly, based on a computer-generated scoring system, and the test can be done manually, using answer sheets, so that feedback can be given in the same session. The computer-based result is, of course, immediate.

Necessary time for feedback

About 20-30 minutes, depending on the use of the test and the level of the testee.

Format/structure of the feedback

The person giving feedback will explain that, according to the official manual accompanying the Advanced Progressive Matrices, they can be used to discriminate between people of superior intellectual ability in one of two ways:

- Without a time limit, they can be used to assess observation and clarity of thinking;

- With a time limit, usually of around 40 minutes, they can be used to assess intellectual efficiency.

At the first attempt, it is unlikely that anyone of even outstanding intellectual capacity can solve the problems in less than 40 minutes, while it is possible for someone to work on them for well over an hour without becoming bored.

In the feedback session, there will usually be an opportunity for the testee to discuss common errors in completing the Matrices, which have been identified by psychologists over the years as:

- Incomplete solutions;
- Arbitrary lines of reasoning;
- Over-determined choices; and
- Use of repetition.

'Incomplete solutions' are due to people failing to grasp all the variables determining the nature of the correct figure required to complete a problem. Instead, they chose a figure which was right as far as it went but was only partly correct, and an essential element was still missing.

'Arbitrary lines of reasoning' was the reason for the error when the figure chosen suggests that the person has used a principle of reasoning which is different from that demanded by the problem. They thought about the problem in a totally different way and so missed the correct answer completely.

'Over-determined choices' are mistakes involving a failure to discriminate between relevant and irrelevant qualities in the figure chosen and when the person being tested chooses a figure which combines as many as possible of the individual characters shown within the matrix to be completed. It seems quite an easy option, which looks most likely to be correct, without determining why exactly. This may be regarded as a form of over-inclusive thinking. (Psychologists have found that many people who are schizophrenic answer in this way, but as people who are certainly not schizophrenic make errors of this type as well, they describe this form of error as a 'confluence of ideas' rather than suggesting that there is a deeper meaning involved.)

'Repetitions' are mistakes made by people who simply selected a figure identical with one of three figures in the matrix immediately next to the space to be filled, which defeats the object of the test and shows a failure to grasp the point of the test.

The extent of the test completed in the allotted 40 or so minutes, when the person doing the test did not know they would be allowed extra time, naturally affects the number of puzzles left over later. So, the total scores from unlimited time are not identical with the scores which might have been obtained if people were allowed to complete the problems as an untimed test. People who, in 40 minutes, attempted all but the last four problems suffered reduced scores. In other words, people tend to differ more in their rate of work than in their intellectual capacity.

Value to the employer/user

Each problem within Raven's Matrices has been devised as a system of thought, while the order in which the problems are presented provides the standard training in the method of working. This explains the expression 'Progressive Matrices'. In this respect, they are invaluable in analysing thinking patterns and the ability of people to grasp complex thought processes. By themselves, they are not tests of general intelligence, and it is always a mistake to describe them as such.

Raven's Matrices are also useful in understanding a person's speed of accurate intellectual work, as distinct from capacity for orderly thinking. Because the tests include simple problems which grow more difficult, a person's speed of intellectual work cannot be deduced from the number of problems solved in a fixed time. It is not necessary for everyone to attempt every problem before stopping.

By imposing a time limit, a person's intellectual efficiency, in the sense of speed of accurate intellectual work, can be assessed. This is generally, but not always, related to capacity for orderly thinking. Knowing a person's intellectual efficiency is useful in assessing their suitability for work which requires quick, accurate judgements.

Value to the employee/person being tested

Raven's Progressive Matrices can provide the person doing the test with new insight into their way of thinking. It can be quite sobering to realise that, according to research on Raven's results, based on people having completed the matrices over a number of years, the capacity to form comparisons and reason by analogy increases rapidly during childhood, and appears to have reached its maximum around the age of 14½.

This ability stays relatively constant for about 10 years, and then begins to decline, slowly but with an apparently remarkable uniformity right through to old age. So it can be difficult to improve performance radically in completing the Matrices successfully by taking them again at a later date. The decline continues at the same rate after the age of 60. By the age of 80, a person's score on the Matrices would probably be less than that of a child of only eight.

Value to the user organisation

The Matrices can help in matching people to cultures where a good deal of strategic thinking is needed, such as the high-risk, slow-feedback cultures and, to a certain extent, in companies with a macho culture. The Matrices can also be valuable in the formation of teams. All teams can benefit from a conceptual thinker, and this quality cannot be readily identified in many of the tests profiled here.

Can the test results be deliberately falsified?

Only by practicing with the Matrices and perhaps learning the results off by heart, but the people administering the test are on the look-out for this, and meanwhile there are many variations in the exercise.

Advantages over other tests

The Matrices provide a very useful insight into conceptual thinking, especially when normed against a senior executive group. The fact that there is no use of language in the test – just symbols – can also be seen as an advantage as it can be used for many nationalities. This test can measure intellect without linguistic capabilities.

Disadvantages compared with other tests

The Matrices need to be combined with other tests to give more insights into the testee. The Matrices are quite taxing to complete and often give the testee the impression of being sent back to school. They don't appear to have high face validity for senior executive roles, and good feedback is needed to demonstrate the relevance.

Tests may be combined with ...

Watson Glaser is a useful exercise to combine with Raven's, especially to add a verbal reasoning dimension, and with the Myers Briggs Type Indicator and OPQ for a more general personality profile.

Static/predictive value

Good, reliable, predictive value of conceptual ability, unlikely to change.

Overall review

Speed of being tested – 40+ minutes timed, perhaps one hour untimed
Speed of scoring results – fast
Cost – low
Range of applications – intelligence test, conceptual thinking
In-house/Out-house – in-house, under license
Basic/Advanced – advanced

How to prepare yourself for sitting this test

Intellectual efficiency, compared with intellectual capacity, is more dependent on physical and mental health, so it would be unwise to attempt Raven's and hope to score a high mark if the person doing the test was feeling unwell. Familiarity with the test situation and practicing the completing of similar tests tends to increase efficiency more than capacity, so those who have done Raven's before will have an advantage. (Of course, the more tests are used generally, the greater will be the incentive for people to familiarise themselves with the tests beforehand.)

However, it is a typical procedure in tests with right or wrong answers such as Raven's Matrices (unlike most of the other tests reviewed in this book) for the tester to ascertain if the person has practiced with these tests before, and they may then decide to give the person being tested an alternative yet similar test. Coaching in test practice and familiarisation is built into the Raven's Matrices, which minimises the advantage that people may have from having done the test before. For those who know they will have to complete Raven's Matrices and wish to perform well it can be possible to practice by finding similar tests, but it is unlikely that you will be informed in advance of the particular version of the Matrices you may be given.

Will this test produce a different result after a period of time?

As suggested above, a person's abstract reasoning ability reaches a peak in early teenage years, so it would be unlikely to be possible to produce an improved result after a period of time. The evidence also suggests that abstract reasoning ability deteriorates, so a poorer result on this attribute could be likely after a number of years.

Contact details: TalentLens from Pearson, www.talentlens.co.uk. Tel. 0845 630 88 88

Downloads: Raven's Progressive Matrices Fact Sheet; Sample Reports

Watson Glaser Critical Thinking Appraisal

Background

Although Watson Glaser, like Raven's, is an ability test rather than a personality or behaviour test, it is included here because of its insight into critical reasoning skills, which can be vital in the selection process, especially when looking for problem-solving and decision-making ability. It is one of the most well-known and well-established verbal reasoning tests, with the version having been developed in 1977 reviewed here.

The aims of the test

The Watson Glaser Critical Thinking Appraisal looks at how people identify, analyse and evaluate problems and issues, to reach appropriate conclusions. It is designed to be used for selection, development and outplacement. It considers patterns of intellectual thought according to five main applications:

- Test 1 looks at inference;

- Test 2 looks at the recognition of assumptions;

- Test 3 looks at deduction;

- Test 4 looks at interpretation; and

- Test 5 looks at the evaluation of arguments.

The format

The Watson Glaser Critical Thinking Appraisal includes five separate sets of problems, with 80 questions altogether. There is a large amount of text to read and digest at each point. The five tests examine these five specific areas of critical thinking in turn, but all have a similar format. The testees are asked to look at a range of propositions relating to a statement, and try to evaluate how relevant, appropriate or valid these propositions are. The new 40-question test (see below) looks at the overall issue of drawing appropriate conclusions.

Range of applications

The exercise is suitable for senior managerial roles, and the Watson Glaser is especially used in selection for jobs seen to require extensive use of critical faculties in thinking and reasoning. As mentioned, it is also used in development and outplacement (and career counselling). Companies using this test are looking for people who can think in a similarly critical way as those already performing well in the organisation. The test can clearly differentiate between the critical thinking capabilities of different candidates. It is often used in selecting candidates as medical directors, law professionals or police officers.

Doing the test

Before each test an example is given, and then it is necessary to consider each new problem and make a decision. The Watson Glaser test is usually allotted at least half an hour to attempt, and could probably take longer if unlimited time was allowed. Around 50 minutes is a popular time to be allotted. A large amount of time needs to be spent on reading and understanding the separate problems of the test. While doing the Watson Glaser test, it is important not to lose concentration. The Watson Glaser is intellectually quite taxing and it can be difficult to achieve a high result without putting considerable effort into understanding each problem in turn. These are complex problems, applicable to a variety of contexts. Many of the statements are quite controversial, arousing attitudes and biases which might conflict with critical thinking skills; testees might have strong feelings about these and lose sight of their critical faculties in the process. This, of course, is deliberate.

Examples of content of the test

(Not possible due to copyright reasons.) However, the example given on the fact sheet is as follows:

> *Some holidays are rainy. All rainy days are boring. Therefore, no clear days are boring. Does the conclusion either follow or not follow?*

(In this case, the conclusion does not follow, as you cannot tell from the statement whether clear days are boring or not. Some may be.)

An overall practice test is available from the test distributors, Pearson (see below).

Time needed to complete the test

A strictly-timed 50-minute session is allowed for the 80-question test. A longer session might give the testee the possibility of successfully completing more questions – but each testee in a group should be given the same amount of time. The published fact sheet explains that a shorter 40-question test will soon be available, which could be completed more quickly – 25 minutes is recommended.

Time to score the test

This test can be scored immediately if the computer-based version is attempted by the candidate. Otherwise the pen-and-paper version can be scored manually, but this is a fairly quick exercise, depending on whether the 80-question or 40-question version has been completed. The scoring is usually completed on the spot.

Necessary time for feedback

Between 20-30 minutes should be allowed, or more if this exercise is part of a selection procedure, when it could form the basis of discussion.

Format/structure of the feedback

The feedback given after the test is related to the overall score, and sometimes according to individual performance in the five tests, the feedback is given one by one. An overall percentile score is given of the total result. It is important to determine the norms by which the person is being measured, and these must be appropriate to their professional role. A large range of normative data is available for the UK.

Value to the employer/user

The Watson Glaser exercise is used a great deal in the selection of people in jobs requiring in-depth critical reasoning, including in Science and IT. There will be a band in which people will be either accepted or rejected, according to a specific percentile score. Those with Watson Glaser results which are extremely high may well be seen as overly academic, but those who obtain low results may indicate a lack of critical reasoning and logical thinking. The test distributors mention that there is no set-up fee or license required for the online version, and the test taken manually can be scored through their bureau service.

Value to the employee/person being tested

Completing this test is extremely useful for testees in analysing their capacity to deal with difficult verbal problems, and can open their eyes to being able to 'read between the lines' in a variety of contexts. Are you logical? Do you assume too much without evidence? Do you think clearly and consistently?

Value to the user organisation

Again, Watson Glaser, as in the case of some of the more basic personality tests, gives sound insight into the ability of a person to perform well in certain cultures. It is highly necessary in companies requiring a great need for high-powered individual intellectual performance in problem-solving and executing a variety of assignments, where lateral thinking is needed.

Can the test results be deliberately falsified?

With difficulty, and probably only through acquiring a copy of the test and practicing, or learning the answers to fabricate results, but if the job requires a certain amount of intellectual horsepower which is lacking in the person attempting it, there would be no point in trying to get through a selection procedure this way, as the job itself would then be too taxing. In any case many varieties of questions can be asked.

Advantages over other tests

The Watson Glaser Critical Thinking Appraisal is in great contrast to the standard personality tests, which really only test the type of person the testee might be, and requires no intellectual input. Here, there is very definitely a right or wrong answer in each case.

Disadvantages compared with other tests

The Watson Glaser looks only at critical reasoning, not other aspects of ability, and this can be off-putting to a person who feels they haven't done well in it. Americanisms abound and all the examples are set in the USA, which can be confusing to the UK test-taker.

Tests may be combined with...

Watson's can be combined with other verbal reasoning tests, with abstract tests such as Raven's Progressive Matrices, and personality tests such as OPQ and Myers Briggs Type Indicator.

Static/predictive value

Good static and predictive value, as the result in the future is unlikely to change much, for the reasons explained in the review of Raven's. Ability in this kind of test may also max out in young people.

Overall review

Speed of being tested – fairly fast
Speed of scoring results – fast
Cost – low
Range of applications – senior positions, sometimes junior
In-house/Out-house – In-house, under license
Basic/Advanced – advanced

How to prepare yourself for sitting this test

This needs brains and thought, so you must carefully read the instructions and gear yourself up for serious thinking. Try to make decisions as logically as possible, not based on instinct. Try to take this test at a time of day when you feel fresh and alert. On the issue of the controversial items, there is a need to rise above these and not get bogged down in the detail, but try to answer all the points in an objective and balanced way. The testee should try not to lose confidence during the test, but to keep going.

Will this test produce a different result after a period of time?

It is possible, but unlikely, especially after the age of 30. Ability to answer the test may improve after doing it a number of times, but it is unlikely that basic critical thinking capacity will change radically.

Contact details: TalentLens from Pearson, www.talentlens.co.uk. Tel. 0845 630 8888

Downloads: Watson Glaser Critical Thinking Appraisal Factsheet "Critical Thinking and Job Performance" research by Talent Lens

DMT

Background

The Defence Mechanism Test (DMT), developed by the Swedish psychologist Ulf Kragh in 1969, has now been evaluated by a number of other psychologists in Europe and the USA. They maintain that the best use of this test, for occupational applications, lies in its ability to help predict success in stressful occupations. This reflects the DMT's background in Freudian theory: Freud, in 1914, said that "the theory of repression is the cornerstone on which the whole structure of psychoanalysis rests". The theory of defences was revised extensively between 1895 and 1939, and was connected with the theories of development, neurosis, therapy, and dreaming, among others.

The DMT is quite different from the other tests profiled in this book in terms of the way it is administered, and the insight it gives into the inner psychology of the individual. It is the most clinical (rather than occupational) of the tests included, but is considered here – as in the case of the other tests profiled in this book – in the context of senior and middle management selection and career development. However, as we shall see, it has other applications, in sport and in military training.

The aims of the test

The DMT aims to provide detailed insights into an individual's emotional and psychological development, and in the occupational context gives a view of your ability to cope with stress, and how you make judgements based on only partial information.

The format

The person undergoing the test is subjected to quite a strange experience, which can be both frustrating and illuminating at the same time. The individual looks into a metal box (like a seaside funfair picture-show exhibit from the Victorian age), called a tachistoscope, which blocks out all light except the pictures it projects, flashing at the viewer for very precise periods of time.

When you do the DMT, you are shown a slide very briefly – initially for a very short fraction of a second – and are asked to report verbally on, and draw what you see. Each person being tested is given a large sheet of paper with 20 empty squares, to be filled in with drawings of what seems to him or her to appear on the slide each time. The way the individual reacts to the pictures is revealed in the processes of reporting, and the drawings in the squares, which become progressively more clearly defined as the slides are viewed for longer periods each time.

The pictures shown in the test involve several points of recognition (i.e., things you can identify and draw). Your perception of these, in timing and detail, is used to show the results indicating individual personality development. Blips on the chart in the final scoring sheet can often be closely matched with positive and negative aspects of the individual's emotional life.

Range of applications

The DMT has clinical uses, and also is used in occupational applications, in senior recruitment and career development exercises. It can also be used in assessing trainees, in their ability to succeed in potentially stressful occupations, and for how well individuals will work together in a group or team. It is especially used in civil aviation, the military, and in high-level sports.

Doing the test

The DMT is a frustrating yet illuminating experience, probably quite different from anything previously encountered, even by those familiar with psychological tests. The person doing the test has a chance to understand how it works, by being given an opportunity for a dummy run. The experience of doing the actual DMT exercise is at the same time slightly scary but fascinating. It is extremely difficult at the beginning to draw anything in the squares, because you can see very little, and you will be some way into the test before it is possible to discern specific shapes and objects. Still, it is necessary to draw something at each showing of the slides, and you should not be embarrassed or restrained by poor drawing ability. You just draw what you can see – whatever you think it is – and this is the revealing part. The psychologist will also ask you to explain verbally what you think you see each time.

Examples of content of the test

It would be against the DMT copyright to reveal the nature of the pictures being shown in the tachistoscope, and clearly this would mean that the test results could then be fabricated. The actual content of the picture is not important, as long as it has a certain number of distinct elements.

Time needed to complete the test

For most people, doing the DMT probably takes around an hour, including introduction and familiarisation with this unusual test medium.

Time to score the test

The psychologist will take the drawings away for between 30 minutes and one hour, and will score the pictures according to the perception of certain features in the pictures at various stages in the test.

Necessary time for feedback

The DMT can be used as part of a six-hour process of assessment for senior managers, and is included in the feedback of the entire process.

When being used separately, at least half an hour is needed, especially in terms of explaining the findings and relating them to the individual's personal background. Longer might be needed if the respondent is concerned about the nature of some of the findings. It must be emphasised that the DMT can produce some disturbing results and needs to be handled sensitively.

Format/structure of the feedback

This will involve explaining the implications of the findings, probably both in terms of the individual's personality, and from the standpoint of his or her occupation. Basically, the DMT provides a set of hypotheses about each person being tested, clearly indicating certain features about him or her:

- The DMT can show the way that anxiety and uncertainty is controlled and managed by the individual, and what level of defences are mobilised as a protection;

- The DMT reveals whether people have 'had to grow up early', with implications for their level of sense of responsibility;

- The DMT records activity or passivity, the propensity to integrate or remain apart, and the level of inner resilience of the individual.

Above all, the DMT – as a psychoanalytic rather than psychometric test, based on one-to-one, here-and-now, not compared with any given population – is significant in terms of registering defence mechanisms, speed of reaction and sensitivity/insensitivity. In spite of only partial information, can the subject hold on to reality? Senior people with a great deal of responsibility need to be able to 'think on their feet', act quickly and exhibit tenacity. Will the person continue to be a good middle manager, or could he or she go further, showing creativity, a high conceptual capacity and resilience?

When top CEOs are undergoing the DMT, the strength of their defence mechanisms are revealed; they may be overtaking others on the career ladder, but can they delegate and trust others? They may have strong technical dispositions, but can they work effectively with others? The test reveals that they may see themselves as tough and assertive, or benign and supportive. They may see authority as threatening, or as sympathetic. Arguably, such qualities cannot be measured, and predictions of future performance made, in just a standard interview situation.

Increasingly, in a number of large organisations in mainland Europe in particular, the DMT is helping senior human resources people to look beneath the surface in a totally novel way. The trend is being picked up more and more in the UK and the USA, after many years of use in Sweden and other parts of Northern Europe.

In giving feedback on the DMT, it is likely that the psychologist will attempt to explain the psychological background to the test. The DMT, according to psychologist Paul Kline (see Further Reading) claims to reveal important and forgotten experiences in a subject's life, using psychoanalytic tools to provoke defence mechanisms, which are seen to resemble Freudian defences, first described several decades ago. The DMT's main applications are now largely occupational.

The DMT investigates the relationship between perception and personality by examining descriptions of stimuli. According to Kline, 'subjects draw the stimuli and label their descriptions. The changes and the transformations in the descriptions of the stimuli are claimed, inter alia, to reveal the defence mechanism used by subjects and reveal the past in the present.' Kline refers to a link between the series of descriptions of the stimuli and the psychological life-story of the person being tested.

There are many questions and doubts surrounding the use of the DMT. Does it measure the defences which it claims to do? Is it able to represent the past? What advantages can be obtained from presenting the testing material/format 'subliminally'? (Arguably, the subliminal presentation does change the nature of the test, and gives access to personality data that could not be obtained by a simple, non-subliminal presentation of the same stimuli). Kline argues that given that defences are widely applicable strategies adopted by the ego to deal with internal and external threats, and that the individual tends to employ the same types of defence in different situations, the operational defences used by the person in situations of uncertainty are likely to be mirrored in certain observable personality characteristics.

According to Kline, the most psychometrically acceptable personality questionnaires, such as the 16PF and EPQ (devised by Eysenck) rely substantially on the honesty and insight of the person being tested, and may thus be unable to take account of unconscious motivation. In contrast, the designers of projective tests such as the DMT have tended to emphasise the importance of unconscious motivation in determining behaviour.

A separate study has been made of the DMT as a predictor of the behaviour of pilots in military flying. In its origins in Sweden, the DMT was developed partly because of the 40/60 pass/fail proportion of students beginning basic flight training with the Swedish Air Force. The DMT helped significantly in the selection stage to define a group of pilot applicants who had either a higher or lower risk than others of becoming failures in their flight training. The DMT helped identify those liable to adjustment difficulties in their work and problems in their relationships with their colleagues. It also identified those liable to show psychosomatic symptoms and flight neuroses, and those likely to be more accident-prone. The use of the DMT in the selection procedure for the Swedish Air Force changed the pass/fail proportion from the earlier 40/60 to 60/40, with considerable career development and cost-saving implications as a result.

Psychologists argue that the defences used by an individual and the extent to which they are used are a stable characteristic of that person, based on personal life experiences. Results from the DMT can be generalised to all situations where the individual defends against anxiety and other stress-related issues.

Value to the employer/user

The DMT can be particularly useful in the selection of employees for particular roles in the company, especially where they will have to make decisions under stress in conditions of uncertainty. There are obvious applications in the financial services sector, and in senior positions with a large amount of responsibility. How would a person react to authority? What would be their attitude to subordinates?

The DMT gets below the surface to a much greater extent than most other psychological tests, but is also more time-consuming and expensive than most, and the point of doing it must be clearly appreciated by the test-taker.

Value to the employee/person tested

This test can give the most amazing insights into your personal development, and can graphically explain the reasons behind having a particular attitude and approach to work. The DMT can explain why you have particular strengths and areas of weakness, and how they might be improved or offset. Of all the tests considered in this book, the DMT is potentially the most mind-blowing for the individual taking it. However, although you may feel that, through completing the DMT, you are laying bare your soul, the understanding gleaned by the psychologist is primarily used to make predictions about professional capacity and managerial behaviour at senior levels, as well as enhancing your understanding of your own personality.

Value to the user organisation

The DMT can be used in team-building, and in matching particular individuals to particular roles. It could also be used in matching senior individuals to certain corporate cultures, but there are probably much quicker and less expensive ways of doing this.

Can the test results be deliberately falsified?

Almost certainly not, because what the person is being asked to do seems unrelated to the overall psychological findings. There is no way of knowing how the test is scored, and how a person could prepare the drawings to show personality facets which were not there. This can be seen as one of its main advantages, especially compared with self-perceived and self-assessed tests.

Advantages over other tests

As explained above, the advantage of the DMT is that it is not a self-report test and the responses cannot be controlled by the individual at all: it is thus impossible to falsify. Therefore, it can reveal previously-hidden traits. The DMT gives in-depth insight into personality (and history of personality development) to a greater degree than most other psychological tests.

The DMT is incredibly probing, and most people doing the test are enormously impressed with the accuracy of the results and the way it is administered; clearly the enthusiasm and competence of the psychologist here is very important.

Disadvantages compared with other tests

The DMT is comparatively expensive and time-consuming, and some executives may rebel against the idea of doing a test which does not appear to have high face validity, which seems strange and may make them feel uncomfortable. They may also feel that it is an invasion of privacy, and that their employer does not have a right know so much about them. It depends on your attitude to psychology, and if you are fascinated by the findings for their own value or inherently suspicious.

Tests may be combined with...

The DMT has few similarities with other psychological tests reviewed here, in terms of probing the individual's inner psyche. Most off-the-shelf tests do not provide in-depth analyses of how individuals think, and especially why a certain person came to think in this way. It is often combined with Raven's Matrices and Watson Glaser to give an overall picture of personality and competence for critical occupations.

As the DMT is really more clinical than occupational, it could be combined with simpler personality tests such as OPQ and PAPI, which would add more to the picture of the individual in a work setting.

Static/predictive value

The DMT is unusual in providing historical as well as current understanding, and is also useful in predicting particularly reliably how an individual will behave in the future, because it is based on researching back into the person's development. This has been one of its greatest advantages over other tests.

Overall review

Speed of being tested – slow
Speed of scoring results – slow
Cost – relatively high
Range of applications – clinical/occupational, selection/career development
In-house/Out-house – out-house, with a licensed psychologist
Basic/Advanced – advanced

How to prepare yourself for sitting this test

You should prepare yourself to be surprised, even amazed, to discover what might be revealed, especially in terms of indicating aspects of your childhood and your emotional development.

Will this test produce a different result after a period of time?

Not substantially, because it is clearly not possible to change your past, but different experiences subsequently might produce a new development within the personality. This is not a test which could be completed more than once in five years, such is the novelty of the way it is presented.

Non-occupational note

The DMT is extensively used by sports stars, and is recommended by the British Olympic Association's psychology steering group. A series of athletes have undertaken the DMT. It has also been widely used in football teams. However, as one psychologist commented, 'it got to the point where the results of the DMT could be used to determine which footballer should play where in a team, and that could raise ethical questions too'.

Contact details: www.interpersona.se – Specialists in psychological assessment for risk occupations – enquiries to aspro@algonet.se Tel. +46 8 665 60 20; also Dr Thomas Neumann, Tel. +33 4505 14372

Downloads: DMT brochure, from Interpersona

Belbin's Team Role Model Tests

Background

In the course of many years of research, Dr Meredith Belbin, the author of this test, discovered nine specific Team Roles which help explain why some teams are more effective than others. All effective teams need to be made up of these, and there are no others seen as essential which do not overlap with these nine roles. The absence or presence of these roles in an individual can be predicted by a test designed by Belbin, dependent on their circumstances and situation at the time (the results can vary). This test focuses on analysing behaviour rather than personality, so as such it cannot be called a 'psychometric' test. Behaviour can change according to work environment, and thus the Belbin Team Role results of a testee can change considerably over time.

Testees taking the Belbin test are classified according to their predominant type, whilst also identifying their second and third type. Although all the team types are equally valuable in a team situation, some combinations are more effective than others. Each of the team types has allowable weaknesses which must be tolerated for the benefit of the strengths that go with them. Feedback from the use of the Belbin test often recommends that testees should concentrate on their strengths while tolerating the weaknesses of their own team types and those of others.

By doubling or even trebling up different Team Roles in one individual, all the nine roles can be represented in a team of three or four people. The most successful team is one which combines a fair distribution of the different team types. Teams that are less successful have a number of gaps and overlaps.

When the Belbin Team Role Model was originally reviewed for this book, it was investigated through experiencing a business game demonstrating the Belbin types offered through a distributor of Belbin products.

Management Teams International is an independent training business, operating under license from Belbin. The company claims that teams can improve their management effectiveness by 20-30 per cent by enhancing the performance of the individuals in the team, and especially through the balance and effectiveness of the team as a whole. Participants on their Belbin courses, they further claim, can improve their personal performance by 10-15 per cent. Participants learn how to build, modify and organise their teams in their day-to-day business activities, which the training firm suggests can improve their effectiveness by 10-15 per cent. In the course of the game, the participants take the test, as do observers and colleagues of these participants back in their workplaces.

The aims of the test

As mentioned above, one way of experiencing the Belbin model is to participate in a seminar based on the Belbin test and exploring its implications. This test aims to help people to have increased confidence in their own strengths, and to recognise and accept their weaknesses while acknowledging the strengths and weaknesses of others, and becoming more tolerant of colleagues previously regarded as unacceptable.

In a practical, Belbin-based team role exercise, called 'Teamopoly', the team role profiles of each team player come through very strongly. The exercise has been designed around fundamental business principles, including the need to cope with the present while managing the future, understanding the role of finance, the value of personal relationships in negotiating and the importance of successful negotiating in business. Bearing a certain resemblance to Monopoly, the exercise was designed ideally for teams of four participants, eliminating elements of chance so that the lessons of success and failure are attributed to team differences more than to luck. There are no arbitrary decisions or changes during the exercise, and it is easy to grasp what is involved while allowing ample opportunity for imagination. The exercise has been tested and implemented over the last five years and has been modified when necessary.

The game gives an opportunity for the teams to work on a realistic business problem, requiring financial acumen and administrative skills, awareness of logistic details, speed of response, quick decision-making, appraisal of a competitive situation, negotiating skills, ability to utilise market research, administrative efficiency and attention to detail, ability to understand exact specifications, understanding of different financial strategies (including secured loans, unsecured loans, and venture capital), and tax management. It requires a rapid grasp of detail and an ability to think on your feet. No one is allowed to work on their own in this game, but has to join in with their team. It is necessary to work to close deadlines, keeping all the issues under control. The game continues for 1½ days, and clearly exhibits the different Team Roles in action.

The format

The test – in one of its forms, as reviewed here – involves attending a two day seminar, in which the team type variants are explained in detail. Before arriving at the seminar venue, the participants have completed self-assessments and arranged observer assessments – where workplace colleagues also complete a profile of the behaviour of the test-taker. The first day begins with an introduction and explanation, and then the participants are divided into groups and play 'Teamopoly'. The performances of the teams are then appraised.

Range of applications

The Belbin team types exercise can be used profitably in team-building and in career development, of middle-managers in particular. It is also applicable to more senior executives, looking at the way a team style links in with a leadership style. The Belbin test is not necessarily used in selection, except where a company has created Belbin profiles for its key positions and is looking to match these with new recruits.

Doing the test

The process of doing the Belbin exercise begins with the classification of participants into particular Team Roles, as a result of their having filled in a 'self-perception' assessment, and having asked colleagues to complete 'observer' assessments. In the self-perception inventory, prospective participants answer a series of questions arranged in seven categories, totalling 10 in each. Each section consists of statements which are apportioned a weighting according to their respective importance, and each section must add up to 10 points (see 'Examples of content of the test').

The prospective participant in the Team Roles exercise is then asked to approach six colleagues and ask them to fill in an observer's assessment sheet, containing two lists of descriptive words. List A contains 45 words, generally favourable; List B includes 27 words, generally negative. The observer is asked to tick the most appropriate words to a total of not more than 33 in List A, and not more than 19 in List B. These assessments help to develop an overall picture of a person's team type. The Belbin model is unique in asking people not just how they would report on themselves, but also in building up a picture of how others see them.

The original research conducted by Dr Meredith Belbin was based around dividing people up into specific team types. In the past, the search for a successful management team has been seen almost exclusively as a search for the right individuals. Yet, arguably, the ideal individual cannot ever be found, because the ideal individual does not exist, and cannot exist. Too many of the qualities in an ideal manager are mutually exclusive:

- being highly intelligent, yet not too clever;
- forceful and pushy, yet sensitive and caring;

- dynamic and energetic, yet patient and careful;

- able to communicate, yet also able to listen;

- decisive and able to make judgements, yet reflective and thoughtful;

and so on.

Also, a problem with ideal individuals in an organisation is that they can be easily lost to competitors, or enter a new field, or otherwise leave the business: investing everything in one individual is having too many eggs in one basket.

Thus, the Belbin concept suggests that the building of a successful team can ensure a range of ideal qualities and a degree of continuity. However, teams can be successful or unsuccessful, and the research of Dr Meredith Belbin since 1969 has, to a large extent, shown why. By studying many teams in action and through using a battery of different psychometric tests, a number of management team hypotheses began to emerge. These were tested over several years, so that ultimately Dr Belbin was able to predict the success of specific teams during business activities (shown in the business game), by simply looking at the team types combination, without even interviewing the members of the teams.

What is the nature of the team types identified by Dr Belbin? The labels given to the different types are: Coordinator, Shaper, Plant, Resource Investigator, Teamworker, Implementer, Monitor/Evaluator, Completer Finisher, and Specialist.

According to Belbin's research and the introductory material given with the test:

Coordinators tend to be mature, confident and make a good chair-person figure. They clarify goals and promote team decision-making, but they are not necessarily the most clever or creative member of the group. They are best fitted to be leaders of the team in so far that they can preside over its combined efforts. Coordinators are preoccupied with objectives and have a substantial degree of 'character'. They are disciplined, authoritative and often charismatic, though not domineering. They are free from jealousy and delegate readily, without pride of authorship. Coordinators see clearly the roles of the other members of the team, operating through consultation with control, trying to keep everyone on track. They are neither too talkative nor too quiet, and are good at asking questions and making proposals. They are competent at summing up the results of a meeting and taking decisions firmly. They play an important role in keeping everyone on track.

Shapers are dynamic, outgoing, dominant, extrovert, and can be highly strung and anxious. They challenge, pressurise and find their way around obstacles, but can be prone to provocation, and short-lived outbursts of temper. Shapers are task leaders and complement the role of the coordinator, who may be seen as the overall social leader. If there is no coordinator in the team, Shapers will almost automatically take charge. They have a great need for achievement and are impatient; they are sometimes paranoid, but do not harbour grudges. Headstrong and assertive, they can show strong emotional response to frustration or disappointment. Shapers put more of their own personal input into each situation than coordinators, and have a stronger pride of authorship. They thrive under pressure and don't mind taking unpopular decisions. They like to move forward urgently to action and are strongly geared to results. Shapers sometimes see the team as an extension of their ego and are intolerant of vagueness. They make the team uncomfortable but achieve results, even at the cost of appearing arrogant and abrasive.

Plants are so-called because they could be planted into an uninspired team to improve its performance. They carry the seeds of ideas, with a strong degree of originality and radicalism. Plants are creative, imaginative and unorthodox. They can solve difficult problems, but they are often weak in communicating with and managing ordinary people. Plants tend to work in unusual and unconventional ways, separate from the other members of the team. They are more concerned with fundamentals than details, and are thrusting and uninhibited in a way uncharacteristic of most introverts (which they often are). They can be offended if their ideas are criticised. There is also the danger that a Plant's ideas may not fit in with the team's needs and objectives, and they may find it hard to explain themselves to those on a different wavelength. Plants can provide a vital spark, but it often needs a good coordinator to get the best out of them. Sometimes they are not good communicators and other team members see them as eccentric or nerdy.

Resource Investigators are extrovert, enthusiastic and communicative, exploring opportunities and developing contacts. They are likeable, sociable and gregarious, with an interest that is easily aroused, yet can be quickly lost once the initial wave of enthusiasm has evaporated. They are good at communicating with people both inside and outside of the company, and are natural negotiators. They bring information back to the group and are constantly on the move or on the telephone. They are ideal salespeople, diplomats and liaison people, and although they are good at new ideas, they lack the radical creativity of Plants. Resource Investigators can get bored without stimulus, but are active under pressure. They keep the team in touch with reality, although they must be encouraged to follow up on tasks agreed. They must be kept on track (or keep themselves on track by planning and deadlines) as they are liable to lose focus.

Implementers are disciplined, reliable, stable, controlled, conservative and efficient. They are practical organisers, turning ideas into actions. They are concerned with reality and what is feasible, and operate in a logical manner with a high degree of integrity, commitment and stability. However, they are inflexible and slow to respond to new possibilities, and can be upset by a sudden change of plan. They like structures and systems, and try to build these when they don't exist. Implementers reject speculative ideas which can't be pinned down. Implementers can be counted upon to do reliably what needs to be done, even if no one else wants to do it. If anyone does not know what has been decided at the end of a meeting, he or she would most likely go to the Implementer to find out.

Monitor Evaluators are sober, strategic and discerning. They are also usually introverted, but stable and aware of all the options. Monitor Evaluators are serious and prudent, but lack the ability and drive to inspire others. Their contribution is measured and dispassionate, and they can stop the team from making major mistakes. They are constructively critical without letting their ego cloud their judgement. They can also assimilate large amounts of material objectively and can assess the contributions of others. They must not be allowed to reduce the energy and motivation of the team – as they can do – yet it must be appreciated that they play a key role at decision time.

Completer Finishers are painstaking, conscientious and determined to deliver error-free work on time. They are introverted, anxious and reluctant to delegate, and are never satisfied until everything has been checked. They have a great capacity for follow-through and attention to detail, and will not start something they can't finish. Although unassertive, they communicate a permanent sense of urgency, and insist on discipline and focus. Completer Finishers are obsessed with meeting deadlines and can depress the rest of the team with their anxiety about details. However, their relentless follow-through is ultimately crucial to the team's success. A team without a Completer Finisher can be doomed to ultimate failure.

Teamworkers are very sociable, sensitive, mild, perceptive and accommodating. They listen, build relationships and avoid friction, clearly perceiving the emotional undercurrents operating within the group. They make it their business to know about the private lives and families of the rest of the team, and are good at communicating concern and care. They can adapt easily to different situations and people, and are low in dominance and assertiveness. Teamworkers reinforce existing team ideas rather than demolishing or challenging them. They promote unity and harmony between the more outgoing members of the team, avoiding confrontation and offering sympathy, understanding, loyalty and support. They may be indecisive, but they can hold the team together and their contribution becomes especially obvious when they are not around.

Specialists are brought into the team to contribute on a narrow front. They are single-minded, self-starting and dedicated, providing knowledge or technical skills in short supply, but their priorities are geared towards their specialisations rather than to the benefit of the team as a whole. They maintain professional standards and defend their own field, showing great pride in their specialisation. They have great aptitude and can provide insight into a rare skill upon which the firm's product or service is based, and command support and respect because of their knowledge. However, Specialists can be seen as working apart from some of the more dynamic elements of the team and can lack interest in other people's concerns.

Returning to the exercise in which the Belbin concept is explained by Management Teams International, when the team types are explained, the 'Teamopoly' game begins. Basically, in the 'Teamopoly' exercise, each team endeavours to run its business more successfully than its rivals and make greater profits. Teams have to explain their strategy, position and result at the end of the exercise. To appear as equal as possible, the teams will have the same number of participants at the same level.

The exercise requires the teams to be composed of those of a similar team role type, to create teams of identifiable character. This magnifies the strengths and weaknesses of the particular team type which predominates in each. The **red team** is usually composed of Shapers and Resource Investigators. The **blue team** is composed of Completer Finishers and Implementers. The **green team** is mostly Teamworkers and Specialists, and the **yellow team** is mostly Plants and Monitor Evaluators.

Thus, the red team is full of aggressive people battling for position; the blue team is composed of dedicated workers who nevertheless lack leadership and ideas; the green team is dominated by amiable Teamworker types lacking drive and decisiveness; and the yellow team is full of intellectuals who work hard without necessarily achieving a result. Nevertheless, any one of these teams can and do win the exercise, and come out with the most money at the end of the day.

The Team Roles exercise, after a discussion of the various team types, begins with a long discussion period and then three cycles of actually playing the team game, 'Teamopoly'. This involves a degree of frenetic activity, encouraged by tight deadlines. At the end of each cycle, teams are encouraged to discuss their progress and their financial performance is posted up for the others to see. The teams are supervised by facilitators, observing the teams in action, and noting the behaviours that are exhibited.

The behaviour of the teams in the exercise is very much determined by the predominant team type. In one particular exercise comprising a mixed group of people from several different organisations, the participants were divided into the four teams and behaved in the way expected from their predominant team types. The red team, dominated by Shapers and Resource Investigators, were particularly keen on winning and everyone wanted to contribute all the time. They were enthusiastic and noisy, and there was a constant shift in the leadership role between the different members of the team. The person taking the initiative at the beginning of the exercise was not the person leading the team at the end. There was a concern about getting a clear understanding from the outset and deciding on everyone's roles, although subsequently people did not stick to the roles they had been given. There was a lot of interest in future planning and negotiating. This team was very competitive, outgoing and aggressive.

The blue team, with Completer Finishers and Implementers, was fairly conservative but keen on getting on with the task in hand. It was operating efficiently but there was little contingency planning if something went wrong. There was a lot of interest in what other teams were doing, and thinking of new strategies. There were some ideas, but a lack of defined strategy with constant concern over the lack of a leader. Similarly, there was no one to monitor and evaluate the ideas, so this team spent a lot of time considering alternatives, most of them impractical.

The green team, of Teamworkers and Specialists, spent all their time working together, never acting independently from each other, and often failed to come to an agreement. There was a certain lack of drive to achieve the objectives and a greater interest in staying together whatever happened. Members enjoyed themselves and became friends, but achieved relatively little.

Finally, the yellow team of Plants and Monitor Evaluators worked in silence on the individual jobs they had to do. They had a highly intellectual approach to the task and some members never spoke at all. There was a concern that everything must be thought through carefully, and the exercise was being taken very seriously.

Examples of content of the test

In the self-assessment questionnaire:

- Section 1 asks, 'What I believe I can contribute to a team…'

- Section 2 asks, 'If I have a possible shortcoming in teamwork it could be the following…'

- Section 3 asks, 'When I am involved in a project with other people…'

- Section 4 asks, 'My characteristic approach to group work is that…'

- Section 5 asks, 'I gain satisfaction in a job because…'

- Section 6 asks, 'If I am suddenly given a difficult task with limited time and unfamiliar people…'

- Section 7 asks, 'With reference to the problems I experience when working in groups…'

The test-taker is then given a list of statements to which to allocate points, indicative of his or her preferences. He or she can spread points across the options or choose just one or two most favoured ways of operating. This exercise is fairly challenging to grasp, in so far that many testees initially misunderstand the rubric during the review of this test.

The idea behind the 'Teamopoly' game, used to demonstrate Belbin, is that each team becomes a company, and has to buy product components from the market and from other companies to make finished products to sell back to the market or to other companies for a profit. The winning company is the one with the most money at the end of the game. Each company has to submit its asset sheet at the end of each of three cycles. Each company is given cash and product components, and is given the opportunity to buy more components by auction or by tender. More components can also be bought from other companies, for money or exchange. The auctions are held at a different place each time, and an important part of the game is to understand, from a series of clues, where the auction is being held. It may be that the testee is expected to take part in this "game", but it might be the case that he or she is asked to complete a self-assessment only.

Time needed to complete the test

Initially, the self-assessment takes about 20 minutes, and then the seminar, including the 'Teamopoly' game, takes 2½ days. The observer assessment would take about 5-10 minutes. Thus, the simple self-assessment takes around 20 minutes, which is normally most people's experience of this test.

Time to score the test

The self-assessment and observer assessment forms are computer-scored, and the feedback is given during the seminar. There is no self-scoring method available; all scoring is produced by Belbin (see contact details, below).

Necessary time for feedback

Within the 2½ day seminar, feedback takes around an hour per person, formally and informally. In a selection exercise, a twenty- to thirty-minute feedback session would probably be enough.

Format/structure of the feedback

Before completing the 'Teamopoly' exercise, each person being tested on the Belbin team types, especially when taking part in the seminar, is asked to complete a self-perception form, and must ask six colleagues to fill in observer forms, as well. These are then assessed in terms of the preferred team types. These can vary significantly between different observers, and of course from the person doing the test as well.

Example

One individual (the author) perceived herself in this order: Plant, Resource Investigator, Shaper, Completer Finisher, Implementer, Specialist, Monitor Evaluator, Co-ordinator, with Teamworker ranking last.

Observers completing the observation forms saw her as, in ranked order: (i) Shaper, Resource Investigator, Plant; (ii) Shaper, Specialist, Monitor Evaluator; (iii) Resource Investigator, Implementer, Teamworker; (iv) Resource Investigator, Plant, Specialist; (v) Shaper, Monitor Evaluator, Specialist; (vi) Specialist, Shaper, Completer Finisher.

The overall ranking of the seven views of the Team Roles of this person was Resource Investigator, Shaper, Specialist, Plant, Completer Finisher, Implementer, Monitor Evaluator, Co-ordinator and Teamworker.

Thus, in this particular instance, there were considerable discrepancies between perceived roles and observed roles.

If the test-taker is involved in the seminar, these assessments then form the basis of the division of the participants into teams. The performance of the teams in action is analysed at the end of the 'Teamopoly' game, according to the findings of the facilitators. The computer-scored self-assessments and observer assessments are then given to the participants.

At the end of the 'Teamopoly' exercise, the teams discuss their experiences and what they have learned. It is emphasised that the team may have lost, but the individual will have always gained from the experience. Although the exercise may be carried out in-house for members of the same company, it can be better to put strangers together, and certainly existing real-life teams should not operate as teams in the exercise, since failure in the exercise may undermine their ability to work together in the future.

Extensive validation has been carried out by companies using the team type profiles and sending their staff members to play the 'Teamopoly' game, such as British Telecom and Philips Electronics. The exercise has already been carried out at Templeton College, Oxford, and in the USA, France, Australia and Scandinavia. In the last ten years, many other companies have found benefits through using this test.

Each testee receives a four-page report from Belbin, providing a comprehensive profile of the testee's preferences for each of the nine roles. Combined with the observer assessments, this can produce an eight-page report presenting a detailed overall picture. Examples of typical reports are available directly from Belbin (see contact details, below). These can be based on self-perception and/or on observer perception. For bulk testing, of 200 people or more, feedback software can be purchased.

Value to the employer/user

The Belbin model is useful in team-building from scratch, although the model ignores the fact that it can be important to have certain Specialists with particular skills in each team too. A team could well need a finance director, a marketing manager and various technical experts, and these may or may not fit into the best combinations of Belbin types. It can be a luxury to have the ideal people to choose from, people ideal for that particular team due to their unique knowledge, but also representing a good combination of Belbin types. Thus it is an idealistic yet valuable concept, and is best used as a team integration device, for understanding the strengths and weaknesses of colleagues.

Value to the employee/person being tested

Unlike most other psychological tests, the Belbin exercise gives people the chance to analyse how they work with others, rather than seeing themselves in isolation. Doing this test makes you think much more about others, and their role in your team, than most other tests. It becomes clear that all team types are mutually dependent, and none can operate effectively on their own. Playing the 'Teamopoly' game is a real eye-opener to the way that team types work in practice, and can significantly affect your outlook when you return to your 'real' working environment. Comments made by participants of the Team Roles exercise include the following remarks:

> "I learned all the things about myself which I have been trying to hide in the closet for the past 39 years, but I console myself by knowing that many other people felt the same."

> "After two days with these people I did find them a pain in the backside. Having had time to reflect on the experience, and realising we were all of a similar type, I now accept that others must find me a pain, too!"

Value to the user organisation

The Belbin concept is very useful in team-building and career development, and could be further developed, especially in terms of combinations of roles. Which combinations can be favourable or unfavourable? Which combinations fit in well in certain corporate cultures?

For example, a Shaper/Plant can be a problem combination, and there would be a need to choose the host culture very carefully. A Shaper/Completer Finisher is a useful type which focuses on the task and is good at leading the project. Coordinator/Implementers can be good at achieving the objectives.

Can the test results be deliberately falsified?

Although the self-assessment forms could be falsified, the observer forms must be completed by others, and it would be impossible to carry out the 'Teamopoly' exercise pretending to be a different team type. The fact that strengths are inevitably accompanied by weaknesses is accepted by most people in the end, and the point is that no one person can be perfect.

Advantages over other tests

Overall, the Belbin Team Roles present an entirely new approach to a dynamic and practical view of psychological testing. It is a novel and innovative idea which is simple but effective, and is still relatively under-used, although now quite well known. The exercise clearly exhibits the value of creating a balanced team and understanding the roles of people in it. It breaks away from the idea of personality tests being exclusively geared towards studying individuals in isolation.

Disadvantages compared with other tests

Clearly, it is not possible to achieve a perfectly balanced team in the Belbin mould in every working situation. Only companies with a large workforce, who are often developing new teams, can experiment freely. Existing teams can be also be modified to leverage the value of combinations of team types. So, this test may be theoretical, rather than practical, for some. Also, the seminar takes a long time (how many managers or executives could give up 2½ days to play games?) and is thus expensive. The team types can be analysed by the use of other tests, and the results can be considered without playing the game, but the game can be seen as a useful part of the process of understanding the Belbin exercise in practice.

Tests may be combined with...

A person's team type and subsidiary types can also be assessed through the OPQ test, which may give a different perspective. It could also be carried out with other approaches to teams, such as Woodcock's (see below).

Static/predictive value

Belbin is very useful in defining a person's current team type and seeing how this works in action, so the predictive qualities are explored as part of the exercise itself.

Overall review

Speed of being tested – slow
Speed of scoring results – slow
Cost – high (although one can do an individual test on their own per person quite quickly and cheaply)
Range of applications – team-building, career development
In-house/Out-house – Out-house at Management Teams International, or a company under license from Belbin can conduct the exercise in-house for a client; as can the Belbin company itself
Basic/Advanced – basic

How to prepare yourself for sitting this test

If you are asked to take part in the seminar you must be willing to go along with the game and 'willingly suspend disbelief' for it to be effective, co-operating with others as required. You must pretend you are in a real working situation. The self-assessment forms should be completed as candidly as possible, or they may conflict with the type in action. You must try and overcome inhibitions and get involved, or the exercise would be a waste of time. It is important not to try and pretend that you are a different type, but just get involved in the game for its own sake. Otherwise, if you are doing the self-assessment test by itself, you could consider the kind of questions you will be asked (see above).

Will this test produce a different result after a period of time?

It may do, if the person has been given different responsibilities in the meantime, but doing the test a second time would give a person an unfair advantage over others, because they would already know how the game worked and would not have to spend time learning it. In terms of the self-assessment, preferences can be radically different if, for example, the test-taker (like the author) moved from running her own business and displaying nearly all of the preferences, to a corporate position with limited opportunity to impact on outcomes.

Contact details: Belbin, www.belbin.com – Tel. 01223 264975

Woodcock's Team Development Approach: an alternative to Belbin

A contrasting view of team development has been presented by Mike Woodcock in his *Team Development Manual* (see Further Reading). This is a way of integrating interpersonal dynamics, and is especially useful in explaining why friction is caused between people. Woodcock concentrates on diagnosing teamwork problems, rather than looking at team types as such. He subscribes to a concept of creating teams based on harmony. This concept of the success of teams is not necessarily widely supported; some users of teamwork models deliberately create conflict and aggression in composing teams, encouraging the criticism and challenging of ideas. Woodcock, on the other hand, believes that if people get on well (have high 'cohesiveness') then the work of the team will be much improved.

Woodcock, in diagnosing teamwork problems, proposes a set of characteristics associated with a mature team. He defines nine characteristics, known as the 'the building blocks of effective teamwork'.

These are:

- Clear objectives and agreed goals;
- Openness and confrontation;
- Support and trust;
- Cooperation and conflict;
- Sound procedures;
- Appropriate leadership;
- Regular review;
- Individual development; and
- Sound inter-group relations.

To understand team strengths and weaknesses, Woodcock has devised a questionnaire of 108 statements, of which an equal number relate to these nine characteristics. In terms of the team as a whole, each statement can be true or false. This reveals the extent to which the building blocks or effectiveness have been achieved. From this point onwards, other procedures can be taken to solve the problems of the team. Woodcock is less interested in team types and is more concerned about how the team works in practice, and can thus be a useful alternative to the Belbin model. Examples of statements within the building blocks questionnaire are taken at random:

- 'Decisions seem to be forced upon us'
- 'We seldom question the content or usefulness of our meetings'
- 'People do not say what they really think'
- 'Some of the managers are not trusted'
- 'There is mistrust and hostility'
- 'Inappropriate people make the decisions'
- 'Help is not forthcoming from other parts of the organisation'
- 'There are too many secrets'
- 'Conflicts are avoided'
- 'Disagreements fester'
- 'The accepted order is rarely challenged'
- 'In this team it pays to keep your mouth shut'
- 'People are not prepared to put their true beliefs upon the table'
- 'We should discuss our differences more'
- 'Our leader does not make the best use of us'
- 'We should take more account of how others see us' and
- 'The organisation as a whole is not a happy place to work in.'

Use of this questionnaire is helpful in analysing common characteristics of teams, defined by Woodcock as building blocks of effective teamwork.

See Further Reading.

Global Competence Aptitude Assessment

Background

This US-developed test has been created to measure global competence, defined as "having an open mind while actively seeking to understand cultural norms and expectations of others, and leveraging this gained knowledge to interact, communicate, and work effectively outside one's environment" according to the published research conducted in the course of the development of this test. It is unique among the tests considered in this book in terms of its combination of knowledge-testing and attitude-testing. There are most definitely right and wrong answers here, and the testee is scored on a variety of parameters on test completion. Developed by consulting and testing firm Global Leadership Excellence, the GCAA is the result of ten years of research and development by Dr. Bill Hunter, based on insights from Fortune 500 human resource managers, international educators, United Nations officials and intercultural consultants.

The aims of the test

The GCAA aims to measure the concept of 'global competence' in a scientific way, looking at the testee's intercultural knowledge, skills, attitudes and experiences of dealing with people from other cultures, as identified from Hunter's global competence research, and presented in the Global Competence Model.

The test looks at the Internal Readiness and External Readiness of the testee, in terms of his or her ability to interact cross-culturally. In terms of **Internal Readiness**, the test measures the person's attitudes that relate to their global competence: self awareness, willingness to take risks, whether or not he or she has an open mind, and if he or she is perceptive and respectful of diversity. In terms of **External Readiness,** the test measures knowledge gained from education or life experience: if the person is globally aware, knowledgeable about world history, has intercultural competence, and is effective across cultures. The maximum score for each is 100, so the testee receives percentage scores on each of these parameters.

The format

The test is completed online, with screens of questions coming up one after the other. As soon as a question is completed, the testee goes on to the next, until the whole test is finished. Ideally, testees should complete the test in one sitting.

Range of applications

The test can be used to identify intercultural competency gaps, from new hires through to experienced executives, and can be used to create effective personal development plans, making use of this dimension. The GCAA can objectively assist a company to identify individuals who are appropriate for global projects or for international transfers, as well as to assist in the development of global leaders.

Additionally, the GCAA can be used to measure the global competence aptitude of virtual teams, and provide managers and leaders of virtual teams with direction. At all levels, it can be used to assess the aptitudes of individuals who deal with culturally diverse groups in their work.

Doing the test

This requires progressively answering each question and moving onto the next. Some are quick and easy, others take a good deal of reading of a scenario, and others are presented with a form of Likert scale (such as excellent, good, neutral, poor, weak etc.). Some questions are very simple, and others are more challenging.

The test includes a wide range of difficulty levels to determine testee aptitude.

Additionally, there are questions based on testing knowledge about regions around the world, including North America, Latin America and the Caribbean, Europe, Africa, the Middle East, and Asia.

Examples of content of the test

The test covers many aspects of intercultural behaviours and attitudes, within the areas of self-awareness, risk-taking, open-mindedness, the ability to perceive and respect diversity in employment, awareness of global issues and geography, knowledge of world history and questions designed to measure intercultural competence and the testee's effectiveness across cultures.

One question asks how a man should greet a Muslim woman. Another question looks at the qualities most important in a particular Asian social context. There is also a series of questions where the testee is asked the most appropriate way of responding to hypothetical yet practical and culturally-challenging situations.

Other questions ask testees to comment on their personal preferences and tendencies. Due to the variety of question styles and potential reactions to particular situations, some sections of the test award partial credit. In those instances, the responses are scored based on their level of appropriateness, ranging on a continuum from full credit for the best choice, to various levels of partial credit, to no credit for an extremely poor answer choice.

Time needed to complete the test

Around 30-40 minutes, ideally in one sitting. If the testees are not able to complete the test on one occasion, they can use the "Save Temporarily" feature and return to the test at a later time. A log-in code is provided for a single usage. If the responses are not saved (as instructed) and the computer is switched off in the middle of the examination, the code will then be used and the testee will not be able to continue. The test developers suggest that a group of testees take the assessment simultaneously in examination-type conditions (to prevent cheating and Googling the answers, etc.) and to make sure that the test is completed according to the requirements. This might take longer due to the necessary administrative arrangements.

Time to score the test

The score is presented in the form of a report immediately on test submission. The testee should have a printer available to print out the report. Otherwise the scores could be written down or saved in a computer file, as there is a lot of useful information in the nine-page report, which includes valuable links and bibliographic material.

Necessary time for feedback

Feedback is provided instantaneously through the individual computerised report, which might take 20-30 minutes to read. In addition, each organisational user can receive a formal aggregate report, once all the testees have completed the assessment. This overview can highlight areas of concern among various employee groups, and can help human resource managers to identify appropriate development programmes.

A user organisation can also consult the test providers to assist testees with interpreting their individual results, as well as providing customised training in how to improve various aspects of global competence throughout the organisation. There is also an opportunity to make use of a 360° feedback version on each testee to balance the self-reporting nature of test. The timetable for these activities obviously depends on the user organisation and the reaction time of the testees to the tests, and of the time taken by the 360° assessors.

Format/structure of the feedback

The feedback is structured around the Internal and External Readiness issues mentioned above, with the numerical results expressed for each of the eight components of global competence. In addition, the testee receives two overall scores, one for the Internal Readiness score and one for the External Readiness score. These scores are explained with their own narratives, combined with two overall ratings of either 'High Aptitude', 'Developing Aptitude', or 'Underdeveloped Aptitude for Global Competence'. The Internal Readiness components include self-awareness, willingness to take risks, being open-minded, being perceptive and respectful of diversity; whilst the External Readiness components include global awareness, knowledge about world history, intercultural competence and effectiveness across cultures. Individuals designated as globally competent by this test need to have High Aptitude ratings for both the Internal Readiness and External Readiness categories.

Value to the employer/user

In an increasingly globalised economy, understanding the global competence of employees can be critical in cross-cultural business interactions, and therefore in maintaining or achieving a competitive edge internationally. Many organisations recognise this, but don't necessarily use psychological tests or exercises to investigate global competence in a scientific way.

This can be seen as a unique test, and it can be especially useful for an organisation with overseas operations, which may be looking to select staff for international assignments, or to appraise individuals and their suitability for such a posting. It can be helpful to both the user and the testee as it can identify competency gaps that may need to be addressed to achieve maximum potential.

Value to the employee/person being tested

This test helps job seekers and employees to consider their levels of interest and readiness for an international career in a more systematic way, which can also be compared with others. Some testees think it will be easy and that they are bound to get a high score, and then they don't. They might find they are competent on External Readiness, but not Internal Readiness – and vice-versa. Most testees find that the test takes longer than they expected, and is more challenging than they might have assumed, so they might then realise that having this competency is not a given.

Value to the user organisation

This test might reveal possible candidates who lack global competence, who could then be rejected for international opportunities for a company. The test creators recommend its use as an objective criterion in an employee's or new hire's appraisal portfolio, and it should be combined with other performance appraisals or interviews. It could also be used within a battery of tests which might test other qualities and competencies for an offshore posting, such as autonomy, self-starting ability, or even integrity.

Can the test results be deliberately falsified?

This could be difficult, as a testee could not take the same test twice, and therefore learn from previous mistakes. If the test is invigilated, there will be no opportunities for looking up answers. Guessing does not mean that scores are falsified. According to the test designers, "there are validity items throughout each of the self-assessment question stems to determine when someone is reporting insincerely. Our data for the Internal Readiness components varies quite extensively among individuals, demonstrating that this is not an issue".

Advantages over other tests

The test designers claim there are no other assessments on the market testing all the components of global competence, and they argue that none is as comprehensive as the GCAA.

Disadvantages compared with other tests

The test designers accept that the version of the test available to date (and reviewed here) may be more suited to Americans than individuals from some other regions of the world. In time, the developers intend to create regionally-specific versions to more accurately reflect different cultural situations around the world. At the time of the review of this test, many of the scenario questions were written within an American context; however, the test designers have since removed many of these cultural cues during the latest test refinement. The test depends mostly on self-assessed attitudes, so the test designers have tried cross-referencing in various question styles to ascertain each of the components from multiple angles, to increase the likelihood of an accurate assessment. There is also the 360° feedback version, mentioned above.

Tests may be combined with...

As mentioned above, this test could be used with instruments looking at competencies, attitudes and other preferences of the testees – such as PAPI, OPQ, 16PF and 15FQ+, as well as a test of emotional maturity and stability, like the DMT. The choices made by respondents at their desks at home might not be the same as they would behaviourally take in the field; but it can be seen as a broad indicator of readiness. With the current high level of expatriate failure experienced by many organisations, a test such as the GCAA could help cut down attrition in this problematic area. However, it should not be the only factor considered.

Static/predictive value

The researchers and test designers expect that aptitude in global competence will increase with work and living experience. The assessment has been designed to determine opportunities for personal improvement for a team or company.

The test measures current attitudes and knowledge, and due to individual testee personal growth, it may not predict how the testee behaves in a future situation out in the field, due to knowledge or experience gained since initially taking the GCAA. This test is clearly not a substitute for an actual performance appraisal. The test designers and many users recommend a post-test to assess the change in a testee's global competence after a field experience or another form of training, sometimes as a means of determining the effectiveness of development programmes.

Overall review

Speed of being tested – moderate, around 30-40 minutes
Speed of scoring results – an immediate individual feedback report is produced on completion of the test
Cost – moderate, through the testing organisation's website
Range of applications – broad
In-house/Out-house – can be completed at work or at home
Basic/Advanced – moderate – questions range in difficulty from simple to challenging, depending on testee perception

How to prepare yourself for sitting this test

For situational questions, testees could imagine themselves as the employee of a multinational, or anyone working overseas. It would seem that the "right" answers relate to exhibiting sensitivity to both the needs of the employer and of the cultural context. There is no clear way to prepare, except by thinking about overseas experiences, when the testee felt challenged about which decision to take.

Will this test produce a different result after a period of time?

As testees gain more experience in the field, it might be expected that they gain higher scores on the GCAA.

Contact details: www.globalcompetence.org, especially Take the GCAA for a sample test; once you have purchased a log-in, go to the site for test-taking, www.periscopeiq/com/takegcaa

Further Reading

Leadership, management and occupational psychology

Barr, L. and Barr, N. (1994) *Leadership Development: maturity and power*, OPP

De Bono, S., Jones, S. and van der Heijden, B. (2008) *Managing Cultural Diversity*, Meyer and Meyer

Devine, M. (1990) *The Photo-Fit Manager: Building a Picture of Management in the 1990s*, Unwin

George, J.M. and Jones, G.R (2002) *Organisational Behavior*, Prentice Hall

Handy, Charles (1979) *Gods of Management*, Pan

Handy, Charles (1985) *Understanding Organisations*, Penguin

Hellreigel, D. and Slocum, J.W. (2004), *Organisational Behavior*, South-Western/Thomson Learning

Hoojberg R. and Petrock F. (1993) "On culture change: using the competing values framework to help leaders execute a transformational strategy", *Human Resource Management*, 32, 29-50

Hollander, E.P. (1978) *Leadership Dynamics*, The Free Press

Jay, A. (1969) *Management of Machiavelli*, Hodder and Stoughton

Lewis, C. (1985) *Employee Selection*, Hutchinson

McClelland, D. (1999) "Identifying Competencies with Behavioral-Event Interviews", *Psychological Science*, Spring: 331-339

Mendenhall, M., Punnet, B.J. and Ricks, D. (1995) *Global Management*, Blackwell

Mintzberg, H. (1973) *The Nature of Managerial Work*, Harper & Row

Reddy, M. (1990) *The Manager's Guide to Counseling at Work*, Methuen

Remme, J., Jones, S., van der Heijden, B., and De Bono, S. (2008) *Leadership, Change and Responsibility*, Meyer and Meyer

Schutz, W. (1979) *Profound Simplicity*, OPP

Smith, M. and Robertson, (1986) *Systematic Staff Selection*, Macmillan

Warr, P.B. (1971) *Psychology at Work*, Penguin

Psychological testing in general

Anastasi, A. (1988) *Psychological Testing*, Macmillan

Carter, P. and Russell, K. (2001) *Psychometric Testing*, Wiley

Carter, P. and Russell, K. (2003) *More Psychometric Testing*, Wiley

Crombach, L.J. (1984) *Essentials of Psychological Testing*, Harper & Row

Herriot, P. (1989) *Assessment and Selection in Organisations*, Wiley

Keirsey D. and Bates, M. (1984) *Please Understand Me: Character and Temperament Types*, Prometheus Nemesis Books

Kline, P. (1986) *A Handbook of Test Construction*, Methuen

Jackson, D., Wroblewski, V. and Ashton, M. (2000) "The Impact of Faking on Employment Tests: Does Forced Choice Offer a Solution?", *Human Performance*, 13(4): 371-388

Martin, B.A., Bowen, C.C. and Hunt, S.J. (2002) "How Effective are People at Faking on Personality Questionnaires?", *Personality and Individual Differences*, 32(2): 247-256

Miller, K.M. (1975) *Psychological Testing in Personnel Assessment*, Gower

O'Neill, B. (1990) *The Manager as an Assessor: A Manager's Guide to Assessing and Selecting People*, The Industrial Society

Semeonoff, B. (1966) *Personality Assessment*, Penguin

Smith, M. et al, (1989) *Selection and Assessment: A New Appraisal*, Pitman

Thornton, C.G. and Byham, W.C. (1982) *Assessment Centres and Managerial Performance*, Academic Press

Toplis, John, Dulewicz, Victor and Fletcher, Clive (2004) *Psychological Testing*, 4th edition, CIPD

Tyler, L.E. (1963) *Tests on Measurements*, Prentice Hall

Specific tests

Bartram, D. (2005) "The great eight competencies: a criterion approach to validation", *Journal of Applied Psychology*, 90(6): 1185-1203

Briggs Myers, Isabel and Myers, P.B. (1988) *Gifts Differing: understanding personality types*, OPP

Briggs Myers, Isabel (2000) *Introduction to Type: a guide to understanding your results on the Myers Briggs Type Indicator*, OPP

Carr, S. (2003) *Finding the Fit: helping clients clarify MBTI*, OPP

Cattell, H.E.P. and Schueger, J.M. (2003) *Essentials of the 16PF Assessment*, OPP

Eysenck, H.J. (1962) *Know Your Own IQ*, Penguin

Freud, A. (1976) *The Ego and the Mechanisms of Defence*, The Hogarth Press

Friedman, M. and Rosenman, R. (1974) *Type A Behavior and Your Heart*, Knopf Press

Hammer, Allen (1993) *Introduction to Type and Careers*, OPP

Hirsch, S.K. and Kummerow, J. (1990) *Introduction to Type in Organisations*, OPP

Killen, D. and Murphy D.(2003) *Introduction to Type and Conflict*, OPP

Kilmann, R.H. and Thomas, K.W. (1977) "Developing a Forced-Choice Measure of Conflict-Handling Behavior: the MODE Instrument", *Educational and Psychological Measurement*, Vol. 37, No. 2, 309-325

Kragh, U. and Smith, G. (1970) *Precept Genetic Analysis*, Gleerups Lund, Sweden

Phillipson, H. (1955) *The Object Relations Technique*, Tavistock Publications

Reddin, B. (1991) *Tests for the Output-Oriented Manager*, Kogan Page

Thomas, K.W. (2002) *Introduction to Conflict Management*, OPP

Waterman, J.A. and Rogers, J. (2007) *Introduction to the FIRO-B Instrument*, OPP

Team testing

Belbin, R. M. (1981) *Management Teams: Why They Succeed or Fail*, Heinemann

Belbin, R. M. (2000) *Beyond the Team*, Butterworth Heinemann

Belbin, R. M. (2004) *Management Teams: Why They Succeed or Fail*, Butterworth Heinemann

Belbin, R.M. (2008) *The Belbin Guide to Succeeding at Work*, Butterworth Heinemann

Hirsch, E., Hirsch K.W., Hirsch S.K. (1992) *Introduction to Type and Teams*, OPP

Huszczo, G.E. (1996) *Tools for Team Excellence*, OPP

Nash, S. (1999) *Turning Team Performance Inside Out*, OPP

LaFasto F. and Larsen, C.E. (2001) *When Teams Work Best*, Sage

Ramsden, P. (1973) *Top Team Planning*, Cassel

Schnell, E.R. (2000) *Participating in Teams: Using your FIRO-B results to improve interpersonal effectiveness*, OPP

Woodcock, M. (1979) *Team Development Manual*, Gower Press

Psychology courses

These are commonly available in adult education programmes, as certificate courses, and in degree courses. The CIPD offers a series of psychology courses, at postgraduate level, looking particularly at 'The Psychology of Management' and 'The Psychology of Organisational Development and Change'.

See also the following journals:

Bulletin of the British Psychological Society

Education and Psychological Measurement

Guidance and Assessment Review

Human Performance

Journal of Applied Psychology

Journal of Occupational Psychology

Journal of Occupational and Organisational Psychology

Journal of Personality and Social Psychology

Personality and Individual Differences

Personnel Management

Personnel Psychology

Psychological Bulletin

Useful Websites and Contact Details

Psychological testing companies whose products and services have been reviewed in this book:

Belbin	www.belbin.com	01223 264975	
Cubiks	www.cubiks.co.uk	01483 544200	
GCAA	www.globalcompetence.org	Email only	
Interpersona	www.interpersona.se aspro@algonet.se	00 46 8 665 60 20	Specialists in psychological assessment for risk occupations
Oxford Psychologists Press	www.opp.eu.com	0845 603 9958	
Psytech	info@psytech.com lpaltiel@psytech.com	01525 720003	This test (15FQ+) also distributed by Team Focus: 01628 637338 roy.childs@teamfocus.co.uk
SHL Group	www.shl.com www.shldirect.com UK@shlgroup.com	0870 070 8000	
Talent Lens	www.talentlens.co.uk	0845 630 8888	

Other psychological testing and related sites

British Psychological Society (BPS)
www.bps.org.uk

Test providers recognised by BPS
www.psychtesting.org.uk

Chartered Institute of Personnel and Development
www.cipd.co.uk

Ralph Kilmann (one of the creators of the Conflict Mode test)
www.kilmann.com

KCP (developers and publishers of psychometric tests, questionnaires and assessment exercises)
www.kcpltd.com

Formula 4 Leadership (leadership development and assessment)
www.formula4leadership.com

PreVisor (pre-employment screening and assessment testing)
www.previsor.co.uk

Practice Tests (online aptitude, ability and personality testing for recruitment, employment and development)
www.practicetests.co.uk

Saville Consulting (developer of measurement tools)
www.savilleconsulting.com

Profiling for Success (psychometric tests and questionnaires)
www.profilingforsuccess.com

Index

G

Hh

Award-winning career coach provides an essential guide to getting that job

Now you've been shortlisted

Your step-by-step guide to being successful at interviews and assessment centres

by Denise Taylor

This book is for anyone that has received a 'you've been shortlisted' letter and wants to feel more confident and prepared for their forthcoming interview.

It covers the different types of psychometric testing companies use, the various forms of interviews they employ, from first interview to panel interview to competency-based interview, as well as all aspects of performing well at assessment centres.

The book finishes with advice on questions to ask at the end of the interview, different ways to follow up and what to expect at the start of your new job.

ISBN: 9781906659325
Price: £12.99
www.harriman-house.com/nowyouvebeenshortlisted